MW01410751

POLIO AND ME

Also by Ken Dalton

Fiction

The Bloody Birthright

The Big Show Stopper

Death is a Cabernet

The Tartan Shroud

Brother, can you spare a dime?

The Unsavory Critic

POLIO and ME

Ken Dalton

2-4-17
To
Pat-Nelson
[illegible]

Different
Drummer
Press

For further information concerning Polio and Me, email the author at ken@kendalton.com

Polio and Me: a biography, a history of the polio epidemics, and the search for a vaccine/ Ken Dalton
ISBN 978-0-692-79672-6

- Polio—United States—History— Sister Kenny—Salk—Sabin. I. Title.

ACKNOWLEDGEMENTS

As I write these acknowledgments, and because it took me decades to compile the information, I have to go way back to thank everone involved:

Doctor Charles Leroy Lowman and the hundreds of doctors, nurses, and staff who bravely stood by polio patients at the Orthopedic Hospital in Los Angeles.

My talented son, Hugh, who turns all my books into miniature works of art.

Wendy Maxham, and the other mystery members of my editing staff.

Dr. Ye, and the staff at Kaiser who saved me from a premature lymphoma death.

All the members of my writer's group, some who have passed on, and those who remain as my stalwart writing support:

Sarah Andrews, Mary Hallock, Thea Howe, Norm Benson, Jon Gunner Howe, Omar Eljumaily, and Dr. Pat Winters

Finally, to my wife Arlene, for remaining my lover and best friend. She took a big chance and married a polio survivor.

This book is dedicated to my dad, Claire, my mom, Virginia, my sister, Pat, and my brother, Richard. I was the one with the paralyzed muscles, but all our lives, and futures, changed that morning when the polio virus invaded my body. My life, and all my successes, I owe to my family.

And to all the polio survivors, and to Dr. Charles Leroy Lowman. He took me, a frightened five-year-old boy and treated me like an equal partner during our eleven year journey so I could walk just like 5everyone else!

Polio victims lives' were forever changed due to their paralysis —a remnant of their battle against polio. This puts people's terror of polio into perspective and makes it more understandable. It was not the disease itself that horrified people; it was what the disease left behind for its victims to cope with in their lives that was so terrifying.
Patenting the Sun: Polio and the Salk Vaccine,
Jane Smith

PROLOGUE

Unexpected questions from two of my grandchildren provided me with the courage I needed to write this memoir.

The first one came from my ten-year-old grandson, Dale, who asked me what I had wanted to be when I was his age. It was an innocent question from a child who, at that moment, was contemplating a career as an astronaut, a fireman, or perhaps a cowboy. But Dale's query shook me to my core as I realized that I did not have an answer. Why? Because as a child who grew up with polio, I had never allowed myself to think about my future other than this single goal: To walk with a normal gait.

Dale's question was a catalyst that forced me to realize that I had managed to hide my childhood memories behind a carefully self-constructed mental brick wall, a barrier that allowed me to move on with my life and forget the eleven years of painful trauma with polio.

But even after Dale asked his question I still could not bring myself to face the frightening reality of my polio years. I backed away from that mental wall once again, but, my grandson's question had created cracks in the wall and tiny glimpses of my dreadful polio experiences began to seep through. Over the next two decades I knew that trying to chronicle my polio experiences could help me to heal, but each time I began to write, I pulled back into the safety of the present.

Twenty-three years passed before the second question picked me up and threw me against that wall so hard that I could not avoid it. My youngest granddaughter, Noel, phoned. After a cheerful hello, she asked, "Grandpa, do you think my children should be vaccinated?"

My heart skipped a beat and the wall that I had so carefully constructed collapsed and my mind filled with memories: That morning when two men took me from my mom's arms. The scalding hot wool strips. The pain from my four surgeries. The lonely months in the hospital. My lost childhood.

I took a quick breath to settle down, and said, "Noel, yes, they must be vaccinated. You follow your pediatrician's advice and your children will be fine." But her question puzzled me and I asked, "Why did you feel the need to ask me about vaccinations?"

"Because some of the young mothers I know have decided not to vaccinate their children."

I shuddered. "Sweetheart, you cannot afford to risk the future of my beautiful great-grandchildren."

She said, "Thank you, Grandpa."

"Thank you for asking my opinion."

I was well into my seventies and far removed from the idea that parents would even question vaccinating their children, so after Noel hung up I did some research. I was both shocked and angered to discover that a growing number of modern parents were deciding that vaccinations, even polio vaccinations, were unnecessary for their children.

Many of those parents cited the argument that since none of the children their families associated with have had polio, or measles, or diphtheria, they saw no reason to put their child at risk with a vaccination to prevent a disease that did not exist. But they were blissfully unaware that the reason they had not seen a child with polio, or measles, or diphtheria was that the childhood vaccination programs conducted over the past fifty-five years had worked, and worked well!

I challenge anyone who has decided to forgo vaccinations to read on and travel with me in my magical Polio Time Machine back to the summer of 1943. But before we start, I need to set the stage, especially important for those born after 1955.

In the early 1940s our nation was just breaking free of the Great Depression which for more than a decade had devastated American families. Even though family life in the early 1940s was better than the 1930s, the citizens of our country had developed a high level of wariness and many could not bring themselves to trust the government's rosy predictions of a better future. Would the feeling of well-being be short-lived? Would unemployment jump back to 19% again, just as it had done in 1938?

Hindsight is 20-20, so today it is easy to look back and note that the depression ended when on December 7th, 1941, Japan attacked Pearl Harbor, and this country was thrown into a world war against Germany and Japan.

But by the summer of 1943, the memory of the Great Depression had faded, life was good for our family, and the terror of war seemed far away. My dad's job at the post office was safe. My mom stayed home, as did most mothers of that era. She took care of three children, did the laundry (a full time job before automatic washers and dryers), shopped for food, and cooked all of our meals. Today, many families have enough discretionary money to eat out on a regular basis, but in 1943, at least in our household, there wasn't a spare dollar, so we ate our home-cooked meals while we sat around the dining room table. Looking back, I find it amusing that the reason our family ate every meal together had more to do with financial constraints than a conscious effort by my parents to build a close-knit family unit.

In 1943, the Internet, cell phones, Facebook, and color TV were not on the horizon. For fun my dad would read Huckleberry Finn to us, or the family would play a board game like Monopoly, or we would all sit around the radio in the living room and listen to the Lone Ranger. In short, the daily routine of my family was much closer to the romanticized *Leave it to Beaver* TV show than *The Simpsons*, a sardonic TV cartoon depicting the dysfunctional family of today.

Did the war affect my family? It did, but early on it affected us mostly in a humorous way. The night of February 24th,1942, just a few months after the Japanese attacked Pearl Harbor, "The Battle of Los Angeles" took place. Air-raid sirens woke everyone in the city and I can remember my dad carrying me into the central hallway, along with a mattress, and we listened to anti-aircraft guns blast hundreds of explosive shells into the air. "The Battle of Los Angeles" turned out to be a false alarm, but the trigger-happy anti-aircraft gunners should give you a good idea of how up-tight our country was just three months after our entry into the war. By the summer of 1943, American forces were fighting the Nazis in Europe and Japan across the vast Pacific ocean, but even with the war raging on two fronts, my dad, who was thirty-one years old, and with three dependent children, felt confident that he was safe from the draft.

Now it is time to introduce you to the deadly polio virus, an equal opportunity disease that killed or paralyzed millions of children and adults of all races, religions, and social standings. Please enter my Polio Time Machine, sit down, buckle your seat belt, put your chairs in their upright position, and we will return to the day when I came face to face with a disease that did not seem the least bit concerned that I was only five years old, nor care that it was about to throw my idyllic childhood into the gutter.

We will travel back to that fateful summer morning when I woke, sweating with fever and partially paralyzed.

To that moment when I tried to get out of bed and crashed to the floor.

Back to the instant when polio drastically altered the bright futures of all members of my family.

The receiving room of Los Angeles County General Hospital last week was jam packed with pain-racked men, women and children and their fear-haunted relatives. Hour after hour, nurses and doctors moved among them, checking symptoms and—all too often—confirming the diagnosis of polio. With more than 500 cases reported already, and with the worst weeks of August and September still ahead, it was clear that Los Angeles County was in the grip of its severest epidemic, save only that of 1948.
***Time*, August 23, 1954**

CHAPTER ONE

Summer 1943—Age 5
My name is Kenny Dalton. I'm five and a half, and a lot bigger than my little brother.
I live at 827 Meadowbrook Avenue with my daddy, mommy, my big sister, and my little brother.
My daddy says I have to know my address if I ever get lost.
I wake up and my PJs and blankets are all wet.
I'm scared 'cause I'm big and don't wet my bed.
I get out of bed but my legs don't work and I fall down.
I start to cry and my little brother wakes up.
Patty comes into the bedroom and helps me into the kitchen.
She gives me an apple.

I want to hold the apple but my hand won't work.
I drop the apple and start to cry.
Mommy comes in the kitchen and gives me a glass of cold milk.
I try to drink the milk but the milk shoots out my nose.
Daddy and mommy take me to the car.
I sit on mommy's lap and daddy drives us to the doctor.
The doctor puts his hand on my forehead.
Mommy holds me tight.
Two men come in and take me away from mommy.
I don't see my mommy, daddy, Patty, or Dicky for a long time.

Today, seventy-two years later, as a father of three, a grandfather, and great-grandfather, the idea that an ambulance team could walk into my doctor's office and rip my son or daughter from my arms is an appalling notion. But this was 1943, decades ago, when polio epidemics killed and paralyzed an average of 12,000 children and adults each year.

I understand that having your child taken from your arms sounds draconian, but in Los Angeles, during the summer months of the annual polio epidemics, as many as one hundred patients a day were admitted to Los Angeles County Hospital. Once the patient's illness was confirmed as polio, those patients were moved to the Communicable Disease Building where they would remain isolated until all possibility of passing on the polio virus to a non-infected person had ended.

And Los Angeles was not alone. Public health professionals throughout the country had learned to act swiftly because when it came to a polio pandemic, the end justified the means. So the abrupt actions of the Los Angeles ambulance crew may have seemed cruel, but the fear of polio, both real and exaggerated, caused even rational professionals to overreact. The moment any patient's illness was thought to be polio, that patient would be rushed to an isolation facility where he or she would remain for weeks if not months.

One of the major reasons a diagnosis of polio was so frightening for my parents and the medical professionals alike, was that no one could predict the eventual outcome of a polio infection for an agonizingly long period of time. While I was in the Communicable Disease Building at the Los Angeles County Hospital, my parents struggled with a list of frightening questions without a way to learn the answers.

Would their son lose his ability to breathe and die in isolation?

Would their son spend the rest of his days living in an iron lung?

Would their son remain paralyzed?

Would their son recover some use of his limbs?

Looking back, those weeks apart were among the most traumatic days of my life. But during that summer of 1943, as the summers before, and the summers that followed, children with polio, and their parents, learned to endure long, heartbreaking periods of separation.

So far, you have only met me, a red-haired, freckled-faced boy of five, but my parents, sister, and brother, are an essential part of my polio story.

Perhaps my mother and father, who eventually divorced, would have separated regardless of my infection due to their incompatible backgrounds, but I'm getting ahead of myself.

My mom, Virginia Bardeen, was the third of eight children born into a family who lived in a large home in Hollywood, just off of Sunset Boulevard. During her high school years, she performed in many school musical productions with sets and costumes provided by the giant movie studios; after all, mom was a student at Hollywood High School! Her father was in the oil business so he was financially secure and the Bardeen household included Grace and Bill, who lived in a small apartment attached to the garage. Grace was the maid for the household and her husband, Bill, performed the dual role of gardener and chauffeur. Grandpa Bardeen was the proud owner of one of the first two of 1937 Cord 812 Supercharged Sedans delivered west of the Mississippi River. My grandfather was so protective of his Cord that he never let Bill drive his expensive car.

Even by today's standards, a family with live-in servants, a Supercharged Cord, and a summer cabin located at Big Bear Lake would be considered financially well off, if not wealthy.

The same can't be said for my dad's family. He was raised in a lower middle-class family in southwest Los Angeles with his mother, father, brother Bruce, and a second brother, Harold, who died in his early twenties. A sister, Clara, died before my dad was born, so his parents named him Clair in honor of his deceased sister.

My dad graduated from Los Angeles High School, the only high school in Los Angeles until 1905. He took college prep courses along with a vocational class that taught him how to run a Linotype machine, which was a large, and very complex device that produced lines of letters by a process known as "hot metal" typesetting.

It is interesting to note that my dad's and mom's high schools emphasized the social differences between the two schools. The alumni of Los Angeles High included famous politicians and athletes, but Hollywood High was known as the high school of the stars. Among Hollywood's grads are Judy Garland, Mickey Rooney, Sarah Jessica Parker, Carol

Burnett, and Cherilyn Sarkisian, better known to the world as Cher.

Following dad's high school graduation, he attended Santa Monica Junior College, where he sang and acted in many of the Junior College productions.

When mom graduated from Hollywood High School, she stood at a fork in life's road that would determine her future. Should she enroll in college, or pursue her dream of a singing career? Against all odds she followed her muse and auditioned for the role of Yum-Yum, the beautiful young maiden in the Santa Monica Junior College production of Gilbert and Sullivan's *Mikado*. She got the part, but before she left the theater, she watched the next audition. The tenor on stage was my dad. After performing a song and reading a few lines from the script, he won the major role of Pooh-Bah, the haughty Lord High Everything Else.

Both of my parents were trained musicians—my dad a violinist—mom a pianist, and they ended up with two of the principle roles in the comic opera. According to my mom, the show was a huge success, and during the long rehearsal schedule, Yum-Yum, the attractive young soprano, and Pooh-Bah, the handsome tenor, became acquainted and they began to date after the show closed.

In 1934, as the American economy slipped deeper into the Great Depression, my dad was awarded his Associates of Arts degree from

Santa Monica Junior College. He had planned to continue his education at UCLA, the school from which his brother Bruce had graduated, but his financial resources dried up due to the depression. Just how bad was the economy back then? America's unemployment rate reached a staggering 23 percent, and in those days there was no safety net for the jobless; no unemployment insurance, and no welfare for the families of the unemployed. My dad considered himself extremely lucky when his father helped him find a job at the United States Postal Service.

Some fifty years later, my mom confided to me that she knew her married life with my dad would never match the standard of living she had enjoyed growing up, but regardless of her drop in social and financial status, they were married in June of 1935.

My sister Patricia Ann was born a year later on April 14. A touch more than two years later, I, Kenneth Rogers, entered the scene on March 9, 1938, followed by my brother Richard Dee on July 2,-1940.

While researching for this memoir, I came across the 1940 U. S. Census, compiled on April 11, 1940, by Mr. Sidney A. Fabermeyer. The record showed that my dad, age 28, my mom, 26, my sister Pat, 4, and myself, 2, were counted as living at 1510 Cloverdale Avenue, Los Angeles, California. My brother, Richard was born on July 2, 1940, so he did not appear on the census form when the count was taken. I am positive, however, that my mom, more than six months pregnant, was fully aware that a fifth member of the Dalton family would soon be added.

Beyond the families ages and address of our residence, the census record also showed that my dad was a mailman with the United States Postal Service, and he had worked 52 weeks during the previous 12 months, and he made $1900 per year, and that our family lived in a house that cost $35.00 a month to rent.

That census record provided with me a rare insight into my family. As I reviewed the above information off a copy of the actual census form, I realized that I had before me a snapshot, a picture frozen in time of my family during the tentative years between the Great Depression and World War Two. The picture was not a Kodak moment, but to me, even more informative.

Sometime between April 11, 1940, and the summer of 1943, my family moved two blocks east and a few blocks north from 1510 Cloverdale Avenue to the house at 827 Meadowbrook Avenue where I contracted polio. Perhaps it was the need for more space due to the birth of my brother. But regardless of the reason our family relocated.

Like most of American families of that time, my parents struggled to make ends meet through the world-wide depression, but my dad's job with the Post Office provided a modest, but steady income. By 1943, we lived in a three bedroom rental house in southwest Los Angeles with a used, pre-war, Studebaker parked in the driveway. I am sure that in the eyes of my parents, our family was bordering on the American dream: three healthy children, a home (even if it was rented), and a car.

But by the middle of 1943, even if a family had achieved many of the finer things of life, countless parents went to bed with the gnawing fear that one or more of their children would have polio by morning.

On that fateful summer morning my parents worst fears were realized. My sister's screams for help had the same jarring effect on my family as an 8.5 earthquake. A moment later, as milk gushed out of my nose, an aftershock permanently shifted five people off their once-solid foundation.

By the mid-1800s, pediatricians were finding small clusters of infantile paralysis in Western Europe and the United States. A village near the French coast, a British town in Nottinghamshire, a rural parish in Louisiana, a farm community north of Stockholm—all reported a dozen or more serious cases in a short span of time.
***Polio: An American Story*, David M. Oshinsky**

CHAPTER TWO

The Search For The Polio Vaccine

It will be difficult for the present day reader to comprehend that less than two hundred years ago, each year hundreds of thousands of men, women, and children died annually from smallpox, diphtheria, measles, yellow fever, whooping cough, typhoid, and polio. Today, those people would be alive having taken vaccines that have been developed in modern times. But like all progress, true scientific breakthroughs can, and did, take years of trials, failures, and honest mistakes before success was achieved.

Let's consider smallpox as an example. It took more than a millennium of trial and error effort and scientific research before Jenner's smallpox vaccine was developed and accepted by the medical establishment to prevent that deadly disease.

The first attempt to produce an immunity against smallpox was called variolation and was recorded a 1000 years ago in a Chinese drawing that showed men scratching matter from smallpox scabs into their skin with the hope that the process would make them safe from the disease.

Variolation differs from vaccination because it scraped actual smallpox debris, scabs and pus, into the skin. A smallpox vaccination injected the less virulent cowpox to provide immunity.

Nearly seven hundred years after the Chinese drawing the treatment for smallpox had not made much progress. For example, in 1684, an English doctor prescribed the following steps in a vain attempt to improve the life of a patient with smallpox: bloodletting, purging, bed rest in a cold bedroom with the windows open, and drinking twelve bottles of beer with spirit of vitriol every twenty-four hours.

In 1721, Lady Mary Montagu imported the Chinese practice of variolation to England, where she had a doctor variolate her two-year-old daughter. Today, Lady Montagu would come under considerable criticism for advocating variolation. The process had some success protecting against smallpox, but 2 to 3% of those variolated died from the disease. However, compared to the 20 to 30% who died after contracting smallpox naturally, variolation did make some progress toward improving peoples lives.

Ben Franklin, who lost a four-year-old son to smallpox, suggested to English physician William Heberden, that he write a pamphlet on the success of variolation against smallpox. The pamphlet would include illustrated instructions on how to variolate a child. In 1759, Franklin distributed the pamphlets, for free, to the American colonies.

In 1796, Edward Jenner accomplished a scientific breakthrough when he vaccinated a young boy with cowpox, a mild disease, to prove that a vaccination with a cowpox pustule, rather than being variolated with a smallpox pustule, would provide protection against smallpox.

By 1802, the success of vaccination over variolation was well established and Dr. Jean de Carro suggested the future use of vaccination for its improved success and safety.

A similar timeline on vaccinations could be described for measles or rabies, but this is a book about polio so this is the perfect time to offer some background on how long polio has been paralyzing and killing adults and children.

For hundreds of years the disease polio was called various names: Heine-Medin's disease, infantile paralysis, poliomyelitis, and finally, in the twentieth century to make writing newspaper headlines easier, the infection became more simply known as polio.

Throughout the 1800s, curious clusters of polio began popping up in Western Europe and the United States. Physicians noted increased cases of paralysis. In 1894, 18 deaths and 132 cases of permanent paralysis were reported in Rutland County, Vermont, by Doctor Charles Caverly, who documented for the first time that polio could occur with, or without, paralysis.

All children infected with the polio virus will display a low-grade fever with mild flu-like symptoms. However, in an estimated one to two percent of polio infections, and for reasons that still remain unknown, the virus breaks through the blood-brain barrier—the wall that protects our brain from bacteria and viruses—enters and travels throughout the central nervous system where it destroys the motor neurons that cause the muscle fibers to contract.

Once the polio virus reaches the nervous system, the damage could be irreversible paralysis, or, if the motor neurons that controlled the breathing muscles are destroyed, an agonizing death.

As our country marched into the twentieth century, annual polio epidemics increased in magnitude, striking down more and more innocent victims. How many? In the United States, the average rate of infection per year jumped from 5500 polio cases through the 1930s to 20,000 annual cases by 1950, and reached a mind-boggling peak of 55,823, dead, or paralyzed bodies across the country in 1953.

Because the majority of the paralyzed polio victims were young children, the frantic search for a polio vaccination became a lifelong quest for thousands of medical researchers.

During June, 1934, the average daily number of suspected polio patients admitted to the Los Angeles County Hospital Communicable Disease Building was a 103 or a total of 3090 patients for the month.
The History of the Los Angeles County Hospital, 1878 to 1968, **Helen Eastman Martin**

The Health Officer of the County of Los Angeles hereby orders that the following person(s): subject to quarantine, Clair and Virginia Dalton and their three children, herein after referred to as the subject(s), is/are quarantined under the conditions specified in this order until September 23, 1943, unless released from quarantine by an authorized public health official. Violation of or failure to comply with this order may result in civil detention, and is a misdemeanor punishable by imprisonment, fine, or both.
QUARANTINE ORDER-Pursuant to 120130 and 120175 of the California Health and Safety Code

CHAPTER THREE

Summer 1943—Age 5—Isolation
I hear the doctor tell mommy I'm sick.
Then a man takes me from her.
I remember mommy say, "Be careful. He's only five."
I want to tell the man I am really five and a half.
That is the last time I see my mommy, or my daddy, for a long time.

Two men lay me on a little bed and put me inside a big car.
They drive around for awhile.
We stop and the men pull the little bed out of the big car and take me into a big building.
All the people are in white clothes and their faces are covered.
All I can see are their eyes.
I don't like the people 'cause they look like ghosts.
The ghosts take me into a room and lay me on a cold table.
One ghost holds me down and sticks something into my back that hurts a lot!
The ghosts take me to a room and lay me on a bed.
I stay in the room for a long, long time.

When I arrived at the Los Angeles County General Hospital, I was given a spinal tap to prove that I was infected with the polio virus.

The spinal fluid verified that I had polio, so I was immediately moved to the Communicable Disease Building in the giant hospital complex.

That was normal procedure—within hours of being diagnosed with a case of polio, most patients throughout the U. S. were admitted to an isolation ward or isolation hospital. Patients were instantly separated from parents, family, and friends, all who were forbidden to visit. They found themselves surrounded by doctors and nurses garbed in white, only their eyes visible. As a result, those feverish boys, girls, men and women, experienced a psychological crisis that at times rivaled the physical assault of the polio virus.

Some fifty years later, my mom recounted to me the conversations she had with the family doctor moments after I was taken from the office.

"Doctor Dearing told me if his initial diagnoses of polio was confirmed, you would lose control of many of your muscles, your reflexes, and you would experience severe and painful cramp-like spasms. To alleviate the spasms, you will be wrapped with strips of hot wool, day and night, and after the hot wool is removed, your limbs will be manipulated and stretched to prevent permanent limb deformities. I was barely holding back my tears when he told me that your father and I should go home and pray that the infection remains in your spinal column and does not travel to your brainstem. If that happened the damage to you could be catastrophic. It could paralyze the muscles of your respiratory system, and you could spend the rest of your life inside an iron lung. All you and Clair can do now is be there when Kenny is ready to leave the hospital."

"I asked the doctor if we should follow the ambulance to the hospital?"

"He told me that would be a waste of our time. If your son has polio, he will be placed in the Communicable Disease Building and you can't visit him until the contagious period has passed and that could be as long as eight weeks,. Go home now and be alert for the telltale symptoms of polio with your other two children."

Frankly, my mom's memory of that day was much better than mine but I was only five and a half.

I don't remember much about the County Hospital where they took me, but to this day I can still picture a man dressed in white putting me on a cold table, holding me down and sticking a needle in my back. Trust me, that brusque bedside manner was not a good way to start a new doctor-patient relationship.

I couldn't get out of bed to go to the bathroom, so when I had to pee, a nurse would help me urinate into a metal urinal. That was something I had never done before. And even worse, when I had to defecate, a nurse would set me on a cold metal bed pan and hold onto me while I did what I needed to do. Even though I was only five and a half, I was old enough to know that going to the toilet was something that should be done in private. So each time I peed into a urinal, or defecated into a bed pan, the event disturbed me. In truth, my introduction to the urinal and bedpan set up a deep-seated aversion to hospital toilet procedures that never went away through all my hospital stays.

But enough about bedpans and urinals. As each polio patient struggled through the fever and muscle pain during the contagious period, the hospital staff started the Sister Kenny rehabilitation protocol with the risk of contracting polio themselves.

The Sister Kenny method was new. Prior to 1942, when a newly admitted polio patient showed signs of paralysis, the accepted protocol was to immobilize their extremities. Their limbs were locked in plaster casts, elaborate splints, or they were strapped onto a Bradford frame.

Today, plaster casts and splints are still used to stabilize a limb with a fractured bone, but once the Sister Kenny protocol was determined to be the superior method for the rehabilitation of polio patients, the Bradford frames were consigned to the trash bin.

Today, I am pleased to say that only photos of Bradford frames remain. For those who are curious, a Bradford frame resembled giant picture frames consisting of four by seven foot rectangles constructed out of metal pipes. In the center of the frame was a strong, heavy canvas that could support the weight of a patient in a prone or supine position. Attached to the four corners of the frame were leather straps that were used to immobilize the four extremities of the polio patient for periods of up to twelve months.

Once the polio patient had been strapped

onto a Bradford frame, that person looked as if he, or she, were part of a torture exhibit left over from the Spanish inquisition transported into a twentieth-century hospital setting. Beyond the obvious psychological damage of being restrained, months of limb immobilization caused muscle atrophy that in many cases was more devastating than the initial polio paralysis.

The Sister Kenny method (much more about this remarkable woman in Chapter Nine) was the complete opposite of immobilization. It involved using moist, hot, strips of wool blankets to ease painful muscle spasms and relax the paralyzed muscles so they could be stretched and hopefully manipulated back to life.

The Sister Kenny protocol was a giant improvement over the Bradford Frame, or the casting of limbs, but for the polio patients there were many negative aspects. The strips of wool had to be heated in boiling water and then wrapped around a patient's limbs while extremely hot. After the wool strips cooled, they had to be removed and then a physical therapist would stretch and massage the muscles of the affected limbs. Added to those negatives, the Kenny method had to be performed on each patient at least four times a day!

For the hospital staff, the Sister Kenny protocol was extremely labor intensive. To meet the demand in many hospitals, nurses would roll an agitator washer from room to room to heat the wool strips. Thirty minutes after wrapping the patient, the now cooled strips would be removed by the physical therapists.

The final negative with the Kenny method, something akin to being trapped in the Bradford frame, there was the real possibility of psychological damage from the scalding wool strips and painful stretching of the muscles. To this day, it is not surprising to me that I still recoil at the smell of wet wool.

All polio patients (and remember that the majority were children) were subjected to multiple daily wraps with hot wool strips, so hot that most patients felt as if they were being tortured rather than treated.

Four times each day, during my stay at the Communicable Disease Building at the Los Angeles County Hospital, nurses would come into my room and wrap my left leg and right arm with hot wool strips. The wool was so hot that I would kick and scream. After the hot strips cooled down, a second nurse took them off and then stretched and pulled my legs and arms. As much as I hated being wrapped with the scalding wool, I remember that the stretching of my muscles was even more painful.

There was a great risk of infection to all hospital personnel working in the

Communicable Disease Building. In 1943, medical science still did not understand that polio was transmitted through fecal matter, so nurses and doctors who followed their normal procedures were in daily danger of being infected by the deadly virus.

In 1934, 196 medical professionals who worked at the Los Angeles County Hospital caught polio during that year's summer epidemic. No deaths were reported, but more than one hundred were nurses who ended up with some paralysis and never worked again.

In 1938, California's Industrial Accident Commission awarded a permanent disability rating to 74 nurses and the following year 36 nurses were added to that list, for a total of 110 professional nurses who were permanently disabled during one epidemic—in one year—in one city.

If working in an environment that could paralyze or kill you constituted bravery, then I would classify all of the medical teams that labored through decades of polio epidemics as heroes.

In addition to the death and paralysis, there were social stigmas attached to the polio epidemics. The Los Angeles County Health Department took extraordinary measures by posting, on the front door of the patient's home, a large white sign with bright red letters reading QUARANTINE, and an identical

QUARANTINE sign was also placed on the front lawn. At first glance, with World War Two raging and her son struggling for his life, it may seem strange that one of my mother's memories of those grim days was the quarantine sign taped to our front door. I recall her telling me the story of feeling humiliated when she watched a couple walking up the street toward our house. When they reached our driveway, they crossed the street, walked past our house, and then crossed back to our side of the street.

Families were sometimes quarantined for many weeks, causing neighbors, relatives, and friends to avoid a house where polio had been diagnosed.

I talked with a cousin, Donna, who provided the following memory concerning the Dalton family quarantine:

"I only have one memory of that time. I recall standing outside your house while my mother passed some food through the front door to your mom. And I have a vague recollection of some kind of written notice on the door about your quarantine."

I had never heard cousin Donna's recollection before. While I'm positive that my mom was grateful for my Aunt Myrtle's help during those trying days, I recall that she and her sister-in-law, Myrtle, didn't always see eye to eye. If my mom felt shamed by a couple of strangers who walked across the street to avoid our quarantined house, I have to suppose that she was completely mortified when Myrtle and my cousin Donna, actually saw the sign.

At this point of my eleven-year ordeal, I was still too young to understand that polio could have affected my ability to swallow, or breathe, or that I could have died. While researching this book, I have learned that, based upon which muscles were paralyzed, the polio virus invaded my spinal column and destroyed many of the motor neurons that controlled the muscles in my right arm and hand, and my left leg and foot. Had the virus decided to travel up my spinal column and attack my brainstem, that path could have destroyed part or all of my medulla oblongata, which would have resulted in the dysfunction of my swallowing mechanism and my respiratory system.

Had that happened, I would have been trapped inside an iron lung, like those boy and girls I saw when a nurse, or an orderly, rolled me past the open door of the iron lung ward. I was grateful that I wasn't one of those children trapped inside a noisy metal tube, lying on their backs, staring into a mirror, waiting to die.

And trust me, few children in the iron lung ward lived very long. George, one of the boys' ward orderlies, told me there was a procedure he had to follow when one of the children died.

His job was to walk up and down the rows of iron lungs, turning down mirrors so that the children couldn't see the dead child being removed from the iron lung and wheeled out of the ward.

Finally, after weeks and weeks of being isolated from my mom and dad, I saw them walk into the room. I was so glad to see them I burst into tears. Mom gave me a big hug and told me she was never going to let me go again. A doctor followed them into the room. I listened while he told my parents that the result of my polio infection was "drop foot" on my left leg, and a very weak right arm, wrist, and hand.

My dad asked the doctor to explain what he meant by drop foot.

The doctor asked me to sit up and hang both of my legs over the side of my bed. I did. Then he told me to lift up my left toes. I tried as hard as I could but nothing happened. I could lift up my left hip and knee, but my left foot would not move up or down, or left, or right.

Then the doctor asked me to grab his thumb with my right hand. I did but I couldn't make the fingers on my right hand close around his thumb.

Fifty years later my mom recalled that day. "After the doctor demonstrated the problems with your left foot and right hand, he told me he was going to send you to a hospital called Rancho Los Amigos in Downey for intensive rehabilitation. I usually followed a doctor's advice, but this time I fought back. I pulled you close to me and told the doctor that we lived in west Los Angeles, near Pico and La Brea, and with gas rationing there was no way we could drive from our house to Downey and back home everyday. Then I asked the doctor if there was any way I could do the rehabilitation at our home. He said it was possible. A nurse could train me how to stretch your muscles after applying the hot-packs."

The instant I heard the doctor say the words hot-packs, I started to wail.

While I cried, the doctor told my mom, "As you can see from your son's reaction, it would be better to send him to Downey. Most parents can't cope with their child's pain during the extended rehabilitation procedure."

Mom said, "Doctor, we will do whatever we have to do to get our son back home."

The doctor said, "Do you have a washing machine with a wringer?"

My mom and dad said, "We do."

The doctor thought for a second and then he agreed to send a nurse to our house to teach my parents everything they needed to know. Then he told them that he would set up an appointment at a clinic on the west side of downtown, near the intersection of Flower and Adams. He told them that the clinic was a lot closer to our home than Downey and it might be a better place because it was located on the grounds of the Orthopedic Hospital where a doctor named Charles Leroy Lowman had developed some new surgical procedures that had helped some polio patients to walk again.

Mom remembered thinking that she didn't know where Flower and Adams were, but she knew downtown Los Angeles was a lot closer than Downey, and maybe this new doctor could help me walk again.

So after two months in the Communicable Disease Building, my parents took me home. But when we arrived, my Mom and Dad found out that as bad as they thought things were, they would get worse.

Mom recalled my first day back home.

"I was laying you on your bed when your father handed me a letter. He looked as if he'd seen a ghost. I glanced at the paper and shuddered. The letter was Clair's draft notice and he had to report to Camp Roberts in a week to start basic training. The realization began to sink in that in less than a week I would be responsible for the care and feeding of Dicky, Patty, and you, my bedridden son who required four hot-packs and stretching treatments every day. At that moment, my can-do spirit dropped so low that I almost called the doctor at the county hospital to see if we could still get you into the rehabilitation facility at Rancho Los Amigos.

"Then I remembered I had four sisters.

One by one I called them and explained the hot-packs and stretching, and that Clair had been drafted and had to report for duty in a few days. Each sister agreed to help me one day a week. Betty worked as a teacher so she could come on a Saturday. Esther agreed to come each Tuesday. Mary would help Mondays, and my youngest sister, Teresa, would come every Thursday. Then I called my mother, explained the situation, and she told me she could help me every Friday. So that meant I would be on my own two days a week, on Sunday and Wednesday.

"Clair told me that he felt terrible, like he was abandoning his family, but I understood the draft notice left him with no choice in the matter. Our country was at war and your father was left with two alternatives—go into the army—or go to jail as a draft dodger."

On my first day back in my own bed, my mom handed me a little brass bell. It was about three inches tall and looked like a Dutch woman farmer. During my decade of off-and-on home convalescence, that little brass bell and I became good friends.

She told me if I needed something important, but only if it was very important, I should ring the bell. For example, if I had to go to the bathroom, I should ring the bell. Then she, or one of my aunts, would lift me out of bed, set me on a blanket and pull me down the hall into the bathroom.

Mom asked me if I wanted to try the bell out. I nodded and rang it. My dad was standing next to the bed, but mom told him she had to do this by herself. She lifted me up and set me on the blanket and pulled me down the hall with hardwood floors to the bathroom. She asked me if while I was in the bathroom did I want to use the toilet? I nodded. She put me on the potty and I asked her to leave. But mom told me that somebody had to make sure I didn't fall off and hurt myself. Even though she didn't leave me, sitting on a real potty was better than lying in bed with the urinal or bedpan at the hospital. When I finished my business, she set me back on the blanket, pulled me back to my room, and lifted me onto my bed.

Mom recalled the days and days of following the Sister Kenny therapy. "We had a washer in our house with a wringer, so from that first day you returned home I kept that machine going the rest of the day with clothes to wash or filled with hot water for the wool strips. The strips were about a foot wide and five feet long. I would toss the wool strips into the washer filled with hot water, and after a few minutes, I would use a long wooden spoon to pull out a strip and run it through the wringer. As the strip came through the wringer I'd catch it with the wooden spoon, carry it into your room and wrap it around your leg or arm. Early on I learned to ignore your screams because I knew if you were going to get better, I had to follow the doctor's instructions and wrap your leg and arm four times a day. Later on, I would go into your room and take all the cold strips off and then stretch the muscles in your left leg and right arm. Based on sounds of your screams and crying I guessed that the stretching was the most painful part of the treatment, but just like the hot-packs, I did what had to be done."

Sometimes, after she finished the hot-packs and had stretched my arm and leg, my brother or sister would come into the room to see if I wanted to play, but I was worn out from the Sister Kenny treatment.

One day I got a great surprise when my dad came home from the army for a couple of days. Before he left, he sat down on my bed and told me I had to be extra brave because he was going far away. Because I was older than my brother, Dicky, I was now the man of the house until the war was over. I asked him where he was going. He told me he didn't know, but he'd come home as soon as the army let him.

In April, 1944, after my sixth birthday, a nurse came to our house. She told my mom that she could stop the daily hot-packs and stretching. To the relief of everyone in our house, including my aunts and my Grandma Bardeen, the Sister Kenny rehabilitation part of my polio experience, the hot-packs and muscle stretching, were over.

The nurse also gave us a wheelchair so I could crawl out of bed, go to the bathroom, and even eat at the table with my mom, sister and brother. The wheelchair was a great help but wheelchairs in the early forties were made out of wood and steel. They were heavy and cumbersome and they were not collapsible like today's wheelchairs. So as much as I loved the wheelchair we had at our home, if my mom wanted to take me to Grandma Bardeen's house, she had to carry me in and out of the car and in and out of Grandma's house.

At this point in my recovery I was beginning to feel like a normal little boy whose only desire was to go outside and run and play with his brother. But as the county hospital doctor had pointed out, polio had left me with a condition called drop foot on my left leg and I still could not lift a glass of milk to my mouth using my right hand. And when my mom tried to help me stand up straight I could tell there was a difference between the length of my left and right legs. So months and months after my initial polio virus infection, the residual disability from polio had made the once simple tasks of standing, walking, and drinking a glass of milk totally impossible.

But that was about to change. My mom called the clinic at the Orthopedic Hospital and made an appointment to see Dr. Lowman. Very soon, we would both find out what, if anything, the new doctor could do to help me walk again.

Simon Flexner, an eighth grade dropout, and completely self-taught, discovered an interest in science while clerking at a local drugstore. Needing a diploma to advance his career, he enrolled at the University of Louisville Medical School—a marginal enterprise in 1887, even by the dismal standards of that era. His entire training consisted of two short lectures. He never saw a patient or dissected a cadaver. "I cannot say I was particularly helped by the school," Flexner recalled. "What it did for me was to give me the M. D. degree."
***POLIO-An American Story,* David M. Oshinsky**

CHAPTER FOUR

The Search For The Polio Vaccine—The Early Days

Polio reached epidemic proportions in the early 1900s in countries with relatively high standards of living, at the very time when other diseases such as diphtheria, typhoid, and tuberculosis were declining. Polio's increase was unexpected, in fact paradoxical, given the prevailing scientific theory that improvements in sanitation would reduce all disease. Later, studies proved that better sanitary conditions delayed a child's exposure to the polio virus until after the child was weaned and that child, having lost the protection of its mother's milk, now became more vulnerable to the polio virus.

Around the turn of the twentieth century, medical researchers began to peel back the mysteries of the disease that swept through big cities or rural villages without warning to kill or cripple the rich or poor.

In 1905, a Swedish doctor discovered that polio was a contagious disease. Perhaps even more important, polio could be present in a person who appeared to be disease free and they could infect others.

In 1908, two Viennese researchers announced that the infectious agent that caused polio was a virus. They had determined the viral nature of polio by running the spinal fluid from a person who had died of polio through a filter designed to trap bacteria. Then they injected the filtered fluid into monkeys and all the monkeys developed polio. The scientific world now understood that a viral infection caused polio.

By 1909, the polio epidemics had grown to the point that medical researchers realized a vaccine must be found. A vaccine for the smallpox virus had been successfully introduced in the United States in 1800, proving that a vaccine could protect a human from a virus. It seemed that developing a successful polio vaccine was just a couple of scientific breakthroughs away.

Unfortunately for me and millions of other polio victims those final scientific breakthroughs took more than four decades, not a couple of months or a few years. Decade after decade, the scientific communities labored to develop a safe and successful polio vaccine, but their results were akin to watching commuters on the Hollywood freeway during rush hour traffic—the drivers were trying as hard as they could, but they made little progress toward their ultimate goal.

Why did the answer take more than forty years? Part of the answer was the lack of funding during the Great Depression in the 1930s, which was followed by the second World War. And researchers did not discover until the late 1940s that there was not a single distinct strain of the polio virus, but three. Those reasons contributed to the delay, but the main cause was the perfect storm of placing the wrong man in the wrong place at the wrong time. The man? Doctor Simon Flexner. The place? The Rockefeller Institute. The time? The early 1900s.

Before the Rockefeller Institute opened its doors in 1902, the philanthropist needed a director to run his Institute and that exalted position went to Dr. Flexner, and he ran the Rockefeller Institute for nearly four decades. Flexner was immediately thrust into the middle of a cerebrospinal meningitis epidemic in New York City where thousands of meningitis victims had died. European studies had indicated that a cerebrospinal meningitis was caused by a bacterium and they developed a serum from the blood of inoculated horses but, during the New York epidemic, the serum had not worked as well as expected. Dr. Flexner was familiar with cerebrospinal meningitis and asked for a meningitis culture to be taken from a meningitis victim in New York. The culture was sent to him at the Institute were he used the specimen to run experiments on monkeys and discovered that the horse serum became more effective when injected directly into the spinal cord of the patient. Flexner's discovery saved lives and that singular success put Dr. Flexner, and the Rockefeller Institute on the map. Coming off his resounding success, Flexner's next task was to determine which disease the Institute should conquer next. In his boastful statement taken from a March 9, 1911, edition of the *New York Times*, Flexner alluded that polio would soon be vanquished, just like smallpox and typhus. He went so far as to offer this prediction; "We have already discovered how to prevent infantile paralysis. The achievement of a cure, I may conservatively say, is not now far distant."

Flexner's 1911 prediction of a polio vaccine was more than forty years premature because he had made two vital research errors, and was unable, or unwilling, to accept the simple truth that he could be wrong.

His first error occurred when he attempted to determine how humans contracted polio. He fed his lab monkeys the polio virus but failed to infect them with polio. After months of failure, Flexner decided—with no further evidence—that the polio entered the monkeys not through their digestive systems but through their nasal passages, and that the virus traveled through a monkeys' nasal nerves directly into the monkeys' brains. His hypothesis proved completely wrong, so one might ask how a scientist of his stature could make an error of that magnitude. Eventually it was shown that Flexner had made a very simple mistake. He had selected the incorrect species of monkey for his polio virus experiments. According to Dr. Tom Rivers, the father of modern virology, "Progress on a polio vaccine was held up purely by chance because a big man like Flexner was using the rhesus monkey. Had he tried another species, the cynomolgous monkey or the chimpanzee, the chances are that we might have had a vaccine that much sooner."

Because Flexner was considered America's top researcher, and the Director of the Rockefeller Institute, once he declared that a blood vaccine would not work, nearly all research to develop a polio vaccine that could be injected into the bloodstream ceased.

In 1916, while most researchers throughout the world followed Flexner down the wrong road in their attempts to develop a polio vaccine, the first substantial outbreak of polio took place in America. As news of the New York City epidemic spread through the country, the public became painfully aware that an illness called polio was paralyzing and killing young and old, rich and poor. To this day, the total number of cases throughout the U. S. from the 1916 epidemic remains unknown, but New York City recorded over nine thousand cases of polio. More than 2000 deaths occurred, and of those that died, 1820 were children under the age of ten.

But producing a workable vaccine remained elusive, greatly exacerbated by the lack of basic understanding concerning the polio virus itself.

Throughout a career that spanned almost seven decades, Dr. Charles Leroy Lowman's techniques were legend and his list of accomplishments lengthy: the first orthopedic surgeon in the southwest; in 1931, the first to develop a surgical technique called "fascia transplants" that enabled some polio victims to walk; and the first in the state to push for special schools for handicapped children. In 1971, the Los Angeles Medical association honored him as the "Doctor of the Century".
***Los Angeles Times,* November 9, 1997-L.A. Then and Now/Cecilia Rasmussen**

Dr. Lowman, as the only orthopedic specialist between San Francisco and New Orleans, saw patients with polio, birth defects such as flat feet, knock-knees, bowlegs and spinal curvatures, chronic bone infections, and trauma residuals. Because the field was so new, he invented many treatments himself including turning a fishpond on the hospital grounds into a therapy pool for children with polio. This therapy pool was in use two years before polio sufferer Franklin Delano Roosevelt utilized the 88-degree waters at Warm Springs, Georgia to treat his polio paralysis.
***The History of the Los Angeles Orthopedic Hospital,* 1911 to 2011**

CHAPTER FIVE

1944—Age 6
I'm six and a half now and the man of the house.
One day my mommy takes me to see my

new doctor. She tells me he will fix my bad leg and arm.
She drives us in our car to the clinic. Inside the big, noisy building are lots of kids just like me in wheelchairs.
After mommy gives me a new Scrooge McDuck comic book we go to a little room.
A lady in a white dress tells me to take off my shirt and pants. I do but I don't like sitting in my underpants.
The lady lifts me onto a table.
I read my comic book and see Scrooge sitting on a giant pile of gold coins.
A man with white hair, a white mustache, and a white coat walks in.
The man smiles at me and tells me his name is Dr. Lowman. He says he likes Scrooge McDuck comics.
He asks me to lift my left leg.
Then my left foot.
Then my right arm.
Then he holds out his finger and asks me to squeeze the finger with my right hand.
He writes something on a paper.
Then Doctor Lowman lifts me off the table and asks me to stand.
I'm scared but he promises me that he won't let me fall.
I stand on my good leg.
I try to stand on my bad leg but I can't.
He lifts me back on the table and tells me that boys with red hair and freckles get

better faster.
I like Dr. Lowman.
Mommy and the doctor go outside and the lady helps me put my pants back on.
Mommy and the doctor come back.
The doctor sits down next to me and tells me that I'm going to get a brace on my left leg to help me stand and walk.
I ask him what is a brace.
He tells me a brace has some metal pieces stuck to my left shoe and those metal pieces will help me stand up and walk.
Doctor Lowman asks me how old I am.
I tell him I am six.
He tells me that when I am seven I will have an operation to fix my left foot.
I ask him what an operation is.
He tells me that while I'm asleep he will cut into my foot to make my foot work better.
I ask him if that will hurt.
He tells me it will hurt a little bit but that it's the only way to make my foot get better.
Then he smiles and tells me that by the time I am sixteen no one will ever know that I had polio.
I ask him how long 'til I am sixteen.
He tells me ten years.
I ask him if that's a long time.
He tells me not really.
Then Doctor Lowman asks me if I am ready to get well.
I tell him yes.

He shakes my hand.
I like Dr. Lowman!

Toward the end of 1942, half of the U. S. automobiles, including our family Studebaker, were issued an "A" sticker that allowed the purchase of 4 gallons of fuel per week. The trip from our house to the Orthopedic Hospital and back used close to a gallon of gas per trip so all other driving had to be kept to a minimum. The country was deep into World War Two and various other products besides gasoline were rationed: coffee, sugar, tires, meat, shoes, cheese, and canned milk. My mom told me that because the kids went through shoes and we needed more gas each week to get me to the clinic for physical therapy, she usually traded her sugar stamps for shoe and gas stamps.

While checking out the cover of an old ration book, I noticed the following warning on the front cover: This book is the property of the United States Government, and it is unlawful to permit anyone else to use it, and persons who violate ration regulations are subject to $10,000 fine or imprisonment, or both.

My guess is that my mom never noticed the warning, or she figured out that trading sugar, or gas stamps, did not exceed the total amount of rationed sugar, or gas. The trade just rearranged who got the sugar, or gas. For whatever reason, among wartime housewives trading stamps was a common place as the sun coming up each morning.

While my dad was in the army, even though he had made me the man of the house, the state of California still wouldn't allow a six-year-old to drive a car, so I sat next to my mom as she drove downtown in our pre-war car to my first clinic visit.

In case you have forgotten, or are too young to know, cars built seventy years ago were a touch more primitive then the vehicles you can buy off the showroom floor today. Here are some examples of what the family pre-war Studebaker was lacking: power steering, power brakes, seat belts, padded dashboards, disk brakes, airbags, GPS navigation, cruise control, surround sound speakers, turn indicators, DVD players, heated seats, automatic transmissions, FM radio, back-up video cameras, stereo systems, bluetooth connectivity, and, that blessing during the hot Southern California summer months, air-conditioning.

However, our 1940 Studebaker did come equipped with a solid steel dashboard, which was located just a few feet from my forehead as Mom and I sat, completely unrestrained, on the front seat of that moving vehicle.

But enough reminiscing about the joys of cars in the 1940s.

Upon completion of the Sister Kenny treatment at home, a nurse had given us a wheelchair so I could roll around the house. But the wheelchair of that era were constructed out of heavy wood, steel, and wicker, so they could not, under any circumstances, be considered light or portable. Nor did they fold up. When the day arrived for our first trip to the clinic, my mom carried me to our car and drove downtown without any idea of how to get me from our eventual parking place to the clinic building.

Today, the building that housed the clinic is long gone and only fleeting memories of the structure remain, but the route Mom drove from our house to the clinic, which we would follow hundreds of times, remains locked in my brain to this day. In fact, if someone were to put me in a car today, and I sat in the passenger seat, I could put on a blindfold and call out the turns: Right off Meadowbrook onto Pico—turn left when you reach Normandy—turn right when you reach Adams—turn left on Flower—and a half a block later, we would arrive at the exact location of the old clinic building.

During that first trip in 1944, while mom was waiting for the signal change, about a block from the intersection of Adams and Flower, the melodic sounds of church bells flowed through the open car window. The notes were coming from the bell tower of the St. Francis church located near the clinic and the Orthopedic Hospital. I didn't realize it at the time, but over the next decade, the St. Francis church bells would become my constant companion that guided me through many of the long, painful weeks in the third floor boys' ward at the Orthopedic Hospital while recovering from four separate surgeries.

But back to the clinic. The building was located on Flower Street, which was a major thoroughfare to downtown Los Angeles before the Harbor Freeway was constructed. Mom had never been to the clinic, or driven downtown alone, so it took us longer to get to our destination than she had planned. In fact, we were thirty minutes late for my first appointment with Doctor Lowman. After our initial visit, she learned that the assigned appointment times were just a general target and I don't recall ever waiting less than an hour, and sometimes quite a bit longer to see him.

Remember that the year was 1944. There was no internet, or Google maps to give my mom a clue as to parking facilities near the clinic, and don't forget, I still couldn't take a single step without falling down like a rag doll. So when she saw the clinic building, mom did what any desperate parent would do. She hit the brakes and pulled over to the curb, directly under a sign that stated in bright red letters, NO STOPPING OR PARKING. She pulled the hand brake and killed the engine. Then mom jumped out of the car and ran into the clinic to find me a wheelchair. As she disappeared into the building, I heard the noise as a car skidded to a stop behind us, and the driver started honking its horn. As more cars stacked up, my mom ran out of the clinic building pushing a wheelchair. All the honking stopped when the drivers realized what she was doing. She lifted me out of our car, set me in the wheelchair, and pushed me into the clinic.

Inside, she pushed me around the giant room until she found an empty spot against a wall for me and the wheelchair. Then she told me to stay put while she moved our car off the street and looked for a parking place. Looking back today, I can't help but smile and wonder what else did mom think I could do but stay put!

As I waited, all alone in a room packed with hundreds of adults and crying kids, I wasn't sure my mom would ever return and I started to cry. When she finally reappeared my tears stopped.

Mom pushed my wheelchair to the end of a long line that snaked back and forth in front of the registration counter. After a long wait we reached the counter. Mom filled out some paperwork and talked with a woman behind the counter. Once we had registered, she pushed my wheelchair up and down the rows of filled waiting-room benches and chairs trying to find an empty seat. While she pushed me, she reached into her purse and handed me a surprise—a brand new Scrooge McDuck comic book. I was on my fourth time through the comic when we heard my name called.

Years after Doctor Lowman first saw me, mom told me that when she and the doctor walked outside the examination room, he explained to her that my right hand was around sixty percent of normal and that he was sure that over time, with extensive physical therapy, that number could reach as high as eighty percent.

My major problem he told her, was with my left leg and foot. His plan was to perform muscle transplant surgeries on that foot. He told her that to fix my drop foot condition he would have to perform one, two, or even three surgeries, but he was positive that my drop foot was correctable. Once corrected, I would be able to stand straight and my walking gait would be restored to near normal.

Then the doctor brought up the last residual problem that remained from my polio infection. From the first day of my paralysis, my left leg, below the knee, had stopped growing and was now three inches shorter than my right leg. The doctor assured my mom that the difference in length between legs could be repaired through corrective surgery, but that the surgery could not take place until the proper time, just prior to my final growth spurt, usually between the thirteenth and fourteenth birthday for boys.

Then he told her that he would return to the examination room to explain his plans to me because he found that when children know, and understands the path ahead, they tend to respond with positive results regardless of the length of time.

After we were done with the appointment Doctor Lowman said goodbye to me and the nurse gave my mom directions to the brace shop a block away on Hope Street.

At the shop, she discovered that it would take them two to three days to fabricate and connect the brace to my left shoe. For a moment, she was concerned that I only had one pair of shoes but then she realized that it didn't make any difference because I couldn't stand up and really wasn't using my shoes.

However, my shoes were not my mom's only concern.

The cost of the brace, plus the cost of the examination, and my scheduled physical therapy sessions were way beyond an Army private's pay scale. In fact, on the day of my first examination, mom recalled that she only had fifty cents in her purse. To her immense relief, she soon learned that the clinic, Doctor Lowman's fee, and all the physical therapy sessions would be covered by the National Foundation for Infantile Paralysis (NFIP), the same charitable organization that would become the March Of Dimes in the late 1940s.

The cost of the brace turned out to be a little trickier, but the street-wise nurse had told mom to tell the brace shop that her son was a patient of Doctor Lowman's and that they were to send the brace bill to the doctor's office.

A few days later when we returned to the clinic for my first physical therapy session, mom picked up the brace bill from Dr. Lowman's office and took it to the NFIP office to see if they could help. They told her that they were sorry but they didn't pay for braces. By that time mom had received my dad's Army pay so she was able to go back to the brace shop and pay the bill for the first of my many braces.

Strange as it may seem, if I totaled up all the monetary costs incurred during my eleven-year medical saga, the continuing expense for my braces was the only major out-of-pocket outlay not covered by the NFIP.

And just how did the NFIP accomplish that financial miracle? I will do my best to answer that question in Chapter Eleven.

So my life in 1944 moved from the daily torture sessions of being wrapped with boiling hot wool strips and agonizing muscle stretching four times a day to three trips a week to the clinic for physical therapy in the warm swimming pool on the hospital grounds. Little did I know that I had landed in a respite of calm before my first summer surgery.

In the mid twentieth century when the polio epidemics were at their zenith, leather and steel leg-braces were quite a common sight . . . leather buckles and straps have been replaced increasingly by velcro fastenings. The steel uprights have also been replaced by lighter weight, but stronger, metals.
https://sites.google.com/site/abasioinfo/Home/history

Drop Foot describes the inability to raise the front part of the foot due to weakness or paralysis of the muscles that lift the foot. As a result, individuals with drop foot scuff their toes along the ground or bend their knee to lift their foot higher than usual to avoid the scuffing, which causes what is called a "steppage" gait . . . Causes include: motor neuron disorders such as polio.
http://www.ninds.nih.gov/disorders/foot_drop/foot_drop.htm

CHAPTER SIX

Give A Boy A Brace And He Will Run

Once the polio virus had finished destroying the motor neurons, the average polio patient's prognosis for muscle recovery, over an eighteen month period, could reach as high as 80 percent for a partially paralyzed muscle, and up to 30 percent for a completely paralyzed muscle. But the major problem for medical professionals was that no one knew how much muscle recovery to expect, or how long that recovery would take for each individual.

In my case, during my first visit with Doctor Lowman, he noted the lack of any evidence that the muscles in my right arm and hand were ever fully paralyzed, so he was able to predict that time and physical therapy should bring my right arm and hand close to 80 percent of normal function. However, because of the total paralysis of muscles in my left leg and foot, he prescribed a brace that would allow me to walk while we all waited twelve to eighteen months to see if their was any recovery from my foot muscles so he could determine the proper surgical steps required to correct my drop foot condition.

But how did drop foot create a walking problem? After putting most of my weight onto my right foot, when I attempted to take a step, my drop foot condition made it impossible for my left heel to strike the ground first, so with each attempted step the toes of my left foot, not my heel, would hit the ground first. To avoid stubbing my toes with each step, I had learned to lift my left knee straight up and then flip my left foot forward. Obviously, that unnatural motion greatly affected my walking gait. To put it another way, walking with a drop foot for the rest of my life would be slow, tiring, look awkward, and make it nearly impossible for me to run.

My brace temporarily fixed my walking problem. It not only provided support for the weakened muscles in my left leg, but each time I took a step, it automatically lifted my left foot so the heel of my shoe struck the ground first. Although the brace was a little heavy, and the leather straps that were attached to metal shafts looked like a torture device leftover from the Spanish Inquisition, it allowed me to walk. For the next five years I was not limited to getting around in a wheelchair, or using crutches. The brace also gave me the freedom to run around the backyard with my little brother, a childhood joy I had lost after that fateful summer morning when I could not even swallow the milk my mom gave me.

A week after my first visit with Doctor Lowman, we picked up my brace. I sat down inside the brace shop, held the brace up and looked it over before I tried it on. The shoe and brace were very heavy. What I didn't realize at the time was that the brace was not only physically heavy, but its weighty cost would drag on our tight family finances for many years to come.

Once I put my left foot into the shoe and cinched my shoe laces, my mom took my hand to make sure I didn't fall. It felt good to stand on two legs. Then, after more than a year of lying in beds and sitting in wheelchairs, I tentatively took my first step.

Before we reached our car, I had pulled my hand away from my mom and began to walk all by myself. Once we arrived back home, eighteen months of stored up little-boy energy broke loose, and I bolted out the front door and ran up and down our street.

In addition to my brace, Doctor Lowman also prescribed a night splint to keep the weight of the blankets off my left foot while I slept.

The splint was shaped like an L and it was covered with cloth. The long part of the L was about two feet in length and the short part was about six inches. Each night, before I went to bed, I would place my left leg on the long part of the L, my left foot against the short, upward part, and wrap a bandage around the splint. I'd start the bandage above my knee and continue down to my foot. By the time I ran out of bandage, I had my left leg and foot snugly secured in place.

Today, seventy years later, I do not wrap my left leg in a splint, but when I go to bed I stay away from heavy blankets that place pressure on my left foot by laying on my stomach and hanging my left foot over the end of the bed.

But back to 1944. I was a growing boy, and beyond the scuffs and other normal wear-and-tear little boys did to their shoes, how often would I need a new pair of shoes, or to have my brace rebuilt?

There were three separate factors involved, so that question is not as easy to answer as it should be.

First, as children grow, their feet grow, so my parents expected to buy me a new pair of shoes every nine to twelve months dependent upon foot growth alone.

Second, on average, boys between the ages of five and eight will grow vertically an inch or two each year. Most parents don't have to consider vertical growth when they buy their son a new pair of shoes. But in my case, as I grew taller, my old brace became too short. So normal vertical growth was the second consideration.

Third and finally, polio had stopped the growth in my left leg. Eventually, it began to grow again, but it took time for the two legs to synchronize their growth rates, and for the difference in length between my left and right legs to stabilize. That meant that every six months, the difference between the lengths of my legs had to be measured and the built-up heel of my left shoe had to be changed by a small amount. Eventually, when I was fourteen and ready for my final surgery, my left leg was slightly more than three inches shorter than my right.

So between every child's normal foot growth, and my leg growth, and the reduction to my left shoe heel, I needed a new pair of shoes, or my old brace needed to be rebuilt, or the build-up on my left heel would have to be changed, every four to six months. This was a very expensive process, and it continued over a nine year span.

Now, just how much did my shoes and braces cost?

The best my mom could recall was, "All I can remember is that the brace cost an arm and a leg. It was a lot more than we could afford. Also, during the war, we had shoe rationing so I traded sugar stamps for shoe stamps whenever I got the chance."

As I previously stated, the NFIP picked up nearly all of my polio bills: the physical therapy, rehabilitation, wheelchairs, home nursing, home schooling, surgeries, hospital fees, doctors fees, and medications, but for a reason I have not been able to learn, the NFIP did not cover the cost of braces.

Here is an actual example of what a brace similar to mine cost a family in 1936, eight years earlier than mine. A leather shoe with an attached leg brace cost a young polio patient from New England forty dollars. That may not seem like much today, but the father of that family was a mill worker who made fourteen dollars a week. The shoe and brace cost that family a shocking seventy percent of its total monthly income, and it would need to be adjusted or replaced every four to six months!

In this particular example, again the NFIP did not help with the cost of the brace, but much of the expense was absorbed by a neighborhood 'sunshine' fund as friends and families pitched in as much money as they could afford.

Why were braces so expensive? Because each brace required a unique build with its desired results set by a doctor's prescription.

Building a brace from scratch began as the brace maker took all sorts of measurements. In my case, he measured my left leg from well above my knee to my heel and noted the measurements. Then from below the knee to my heel. Then from my ankle to my heel. Finally he measured the size of my foot. Then, he rechecked his measurements. He kept the left shoe from my new pair of high-top leather lace-up shoes and he told us to return in three days.

The craftsman attached a piece of steel, about a half inch thick, to the heel of the shoe which in those days was made out of leather like the tops of the shoes.

At my ankle, he installed a bearing on each side that would allow the steel shafts to flex with the motion of my foot as I walked. The steel shafts continued up my leg to the spot he had measured just below my knee. There, he connected the shafts to a two-inch leather strap that fit around my leg.

Above the leather strap, the shafts continued up to a second bearing, level with my knee, so that my knee could bend.

Finally, a couple of inches above my knee, the brace maker cut the steel shafts and connected them to a second two-inch leather strap. Both straps, above and below the knee, were equipped with a belt and buckle assembly, so the brace could be cinched to the leg.

Today, form-fitting light plastic has replaced steel, and Velcro substitutes for the leather straps, so the modern brace is much lighter. But seven decades after my first brace, a skilled craftsman is still required to construct each unique orthopedic device.

When I hit the ripe old age of seventy, I agreed, on the advice of my doctor, to have a brace made for me to use when I play golf because I want to walk the eighteen holes rather than having to ride in a cart.

This time around, I went to an orthopedic brace shop in a nearby city and after some initial measurements, the craftsman took a plaster impression of my left leg, ankle, and foot.

He converted the impression into a mold, and a week later, I picked up a light plastic brace that I attached to my leg with two velcro straps. The brace fits my leg, my ankle, and my foot perfectly, and it cost $911.82. So even a modern brace made using plastic and velcro as compared to steel and leather still costs a lot because each brace is a hand-made, unique device, designed to accomplish a specific assignment.

Today, when I play golf, my new brace provides my left leg with greater stability, but I am sorry to report that it hasn't done much to improve my golf scores.

During my childhood days of steel and leather, I can recall getting out of bed each morning, taking off my splint, and putting on a pair of socks and my brace. Very quickly, this morning ritual became as normal as eating breakfast or brushing my teeth, and I was grateful that I had the brace because I knew that without it, I would be confined to bed, a wheelchair, or crutches.

Up to this point I hadn't mentioned crutches because I only used them when I had to. I learned how to use crutches when I was six. Moving from point A to B was easy but figuring out how to go up, or down stairs was difficult. The crutches mantra for stairs goes like this—up with the good and down with the bad. That meant to go up stairs you had to place your good leg on the "up stair" and using your crutches, you lifted the rest of your body up one stair. To go down stairs, you place your crutches, and your bad leg on the "down stair" and then you would lower the rest of your body down to the lower stair. After my last surgery, the combination of crutches and a school building full of stairs was the reason I had to change junior high schools. Just imagine hundreds of teen-age kids running up and down stairs and somehow avoiding a boy on crutches who is mumbling, "Up with the good.

Or down with the bad."

Beyond the stairs problem, using crutches after my surgeries was not a problem, except for the potential wear and tear on my armpits. I'm sure you've noticed that most people you see using crutches have a rubber cover on the part of the crutch that's placed under their arm. Take it from a man with experience, if you want your armpits to remain unscathed, don't assume that rubber covers are only for the wimps.

But enough about crutches. How much, if at all, did my brace limit me? Could I run? Play sports? Could I do all the things a young, energetic boy wanted to do?

Well . . . sort of. While in high school, I never played a team sport such as baseball or basketball, but at elementary school I played tetherball, dodgeball, and kickball, and I climbed on the monkey bars.

At home I spent my after school hours playing handball, by myself, against our garage door. I would make up elaborate games, with formidable opponents and the best player was named Mulligan Stew. Why Mulligan Stew? I haven't a clue, but as good a handball player as Mulligan Stew was, I almost always beat him, usually on one final shot that he couldn't return. During those hours, I was a world class handball player!

I didn't have many friends in the neighborhood. There were some boys close to my age who lived nearby, but I didn't play with them much, though that may have had more to do with my introverted makeup rather than their reactions to my brace. On the other hand, in 1947, when I was nine years old and we lived in the states of Wyoming and Virginia, none of the kids knew why I wore a brace, and I played with, and made friends with other boys, both at school and at home.

Then again, in Wyoming, we lived on the Army base where my father was a first lieutenant, and his rank in the army had more to do with the kids I played with than the brace on my leg.

The base commander held the rank of colonel and as such, his family was the highest ranking family at Fort Warren. The army pecking-order would never allow Colonel Barnaby's daughter to play with a first lieutenant's daughter. The same protocol existed for the families of majors and captains, all of whom ranked above my father.

I have been asked if wearing a brace as a child bothered me. Even at the young age of six I understood that I needed to wear a brace to walk, so because of that, wearing the thing wasn't a bother. In fact, the steel and leather device became a part of the muscles and bones that made up my left leg.

As I look back, it wasn't the brace that bugged me as much as having to wear high-topped leather shoes. All the boys at school, except me, wore low-top leather shoes or tennis shoes. I was the only kid on the playground with high-topped shoes, and as far as I was concerned, every kid within a hundred miles knew that I was the only kid in Los Angeles who wore high-topped shoes.

Back then, all the boys wore blue jeans, not the Levi's 501s that now cost $60 a pair, but regular, good-old blue jeans. My mom like all other moms of that era bought blue jeans with the legs as long as possible so that they'd fit for as much time as possible on their growing sons. Because the jeans started out too long, all the boys at school had turned-up cuffs, sometimes turned up as high as six inches, and because that was the style, the higher the turn, the better. In my case, I kept my jeans down as close to my shoe laces as possible to hide my brace and high-topped shoes. That meant my cuffs were always a lot shorter than the other guys' cuffs. I was not only the guy who wore a brace and high-top shoes, I was the kid who didn't conform with the blue jean style of the day.

Long after I stopped wearing my brace, I still had to wear leather shoes to accommodate my built-up heel, but at long last I could wear low-tops.

The bottom line? I couldn't run as fast as the boys who wore tennis shoes, but regardless of my brace, I still ran around and played with other kids, and after five long years, my brace was gone and most of the boys at school stopped calling me gimp.

All of this could have been avoided if a vaccine for polio had been developed earlier.

By passing polio virus repeatedly through the brains and spinal columns of his monkeys, Flexner produced a strain—known as MV or mixed virus—that was highly neurotropic, able to multiply only in nervous tissue. . . . Given Flexner's prominence, MV quickly became the strain of choice in the polio field, leading researchers down yet another blind alley.
***POLIO-An American Story,* David M. Oshinsky**

CHAPTER SEVEN

The Search For The Polio Vaccine—Hindered Progress

Once the Rockefeller Institute determined that their rhesus monkeys could not become infected with polio by ingesting the virus, the researchers compounded their original error by injecting the virus into the monkeys brain or spinal column, the only way they knew how to infect their monkeys with polio. Thus, the Rockefeller Institute led the world's scientific community to conclude that the polio virus did not enter the human body through the digestive system, and nearly all polio research continued down the wrong path for more than three decades.

But how could injecting the polio virus directly into a monkey's brain slow down the polio vaccine progress for thirty years?

By continually using the brain injection method, the Rockefeller Institute produced a new polio virus strain, known throughout the scientific world as mixed virus (MV). It turned out that MV was only able to multiply in animal nervous tissue and animal nervous tissue can provoke a serious allergic reaction in humans.

The quest for a polio vaccine had run into a brick wall. A vaccine produced from the MV strain could cause a serious allergic reaction, but the only way researchers knew how to make a polio vaccine was from the MV strain.

To sum up, if researchers wanted to produce a successful polio vaccine they had to use something other than the Rockefeller Institute MV strain, but the MV strain was the only polio virus widely available for research.

In addition to the MV obstacle, it was not until the latter part of the 1930s that researchers discovered there was more than one strain of polio virus, and it wasn't until the 1940s that they determined that there were a total of three strains.

In 1935, frustrated with the growing polio epidemics and the lack of research progress, two teams outside the shadow of the Rockefeller Institute found themselves locked in a race to develop the first polio vaccine. Using what some of today's researchers would call kitchen chemistry, the two teams, perhaps looking toward an eventual Nobel prize, or fearing that others would succeed first, rushed their untested vaccines into premature trials.

Today, both of the 1935 vaccines would be considered quite primitive because the developers of the vaccines did not know there were multiple strains of the polio virus. The vaccines were also compounded using substandard lab techniques, but that did not stop Dr. Maurice Brodie and Dr. John Kollmer from going ahead with their trials.

One of the vaccines was developed at New York University under the tutelage of Dr. William Park who had set up a polio research lab. Dr. Maurice Brodie, a Canadian, who worked in Park's lab, came up with a vaccine that consisted of an emulsion of the ground-up spinal cords of infected monkeys. He attempted to deactivate the virus by exposing it to formalin (a formaldehyde mixture) and tested his vaccine on chimpanzees, and then on himself. Finally he enrolled thousands of individuals, young and old, in his trial. In today's modern world of computers and precise data collection, this undisciplined approach to research is hard to imagine, and the actual results of Brodie's trial remain unclear. Beyond a few anecdotal stories that children developed abscesses at the site of the injection, or that some children who had been well before they received the vaccine became ill, all we really know is that after the initial trial, Brodie's vaccine was never used again.

Meanwhile, Dr. John Kollmer of Temple University in Philadelphia, developed a polio virus vaccine. Kollmer's idea was to use live, but slightly weakened (attenuated) virus, again taken from the spinal cords of infected monkeys. The virus was attenuated by mixing it with various chemicals and refrigerating it for two weeks. After trying his vaccine on a few monkeys, himself, his children, and twenty-two other people, Kollmer was optimistic enough to distribute thousands of doses to physicians across the country. Unfortunately, the vaccine did not protect people from polio. In fact, Kollmer's trial proved to be a disaster. Many suffered allergic reactions, others became paralyzed, and there were several deaths from polio, all attributed to the Kollmer vaccine.

There were two other bizarre incidences in the 1930s that indicate just how far the scientific community had veered from developing a successful vaccine.

Once the Rockefeller Institute had incorrectly determined that the polio virus did not enter humans through their digestive tract, scientists searched for another way the virus might reach the brain. Some experiments at the Rockefeller Institute indicated that when a rhesus monkey's olfactory nerves were cut, the polio virus appeared to be blocked from entering the brain due to the fact that the virus' path to the brain had been cut off. From that single flawed conclusion, the watchword among the scientific community became, "protect the nose and prevent polio."

Obviously, no one was going to allow researchers to sever the olfactory nerves of millions of America's children, but scientists were eager to determine if by deadening the human nasal passage with a substance, they could chemically cut off polio's path to the brain.

So trials were organized in Tennessee, Alabama, and Mississippi to spray the nasal passages of 4600 children and adults using an alum-picric acid, a solution designed to prevent the virus from traveling along the olfactory nerves to the brain. The results of the trial were discouraging because researchers discovered that the process of administering the alum-picric acid spray had to be done by experts who understood nasal anatomy. The alum-picric acid spray also had to be strong enough to produce the total loss of smell (anosmia).

The trial immediately ran into problems because they lacked the experts required to properly spray the alum-picric acid. Also, poor data collection made it impossible to determine if the trial produced a positive or negative result.

But the lack of success in the 1936 Southern trial did not slow down the "protect the nose" theorists. In 1937, during a polio epidemic in Toronto, Canada, nose and throat specialists sprayed the noses of 5000 children not once but twice, with a solution of one percent zinc sulfate and one-half a percent of Pontocaine. Even though the Canadian trial used professional otolaryngologists to administer the spray in special clinics, the results of the trial clearly demonstrated that the nasal spray was ineffective as a polio preventive. Eleven cases of polio were reported among the group who received the zinc sulfate solution as compared to nineteen cases of polio that occurred in the control group, indicating that the differences of the polio rates between groups were not statistically significant.

In addition, a temporary anosmia was expected, but six months after the completion of the trial, approximately twenty-five percent of the children had not regained their sense of smell.

When researchers combined the paralysis and deaths that occurred after the 1935 Brodie and Kollmer vaccine fiascos, and the "protect the nose and prevent polio" disaster, the scientific community became gun shy. It took nearly twenty years before they developed vaccines in which they had enough confidence to attempt another polio vaccine trial on human beings.

Thankfully, by the early 1940s, the broad community of scientific researchers seeking a polio vaccine were beginning to see a light at the end of the tunnel.

The identification of the three separate strains of polio virus was an important piece to the puzzle, but another scientific breakthrough occurred during a 1943 polio epidemic in New Haven, Connecticut. A member of Yale's polio research unit, Dr. Dorothy Horstmann, made an astounding discovery that totally debunked Flexner's thirty-year-old theory that polio infected its victims through their nasal passages.

Most scientists believed that Dr. Horstmann was wasting her time in a New Haven hospital looking for evidence of the polio virus in the blood of one hundred and eleven polio patients. The majority of polio researchers in the world were positive that a blood test for the virus would come up negative. They were sure that she would not find any evidence of the polio virus because no one ever had.

But Dr. Horstmann forged ahead and performed those one hundred and eleven blood tests. After reviewing all one hundred and eleven samples she spotted the polio virus in the blood sample from a nine-year-old girl.

Some researchers might have considered her testing procedure faulty, or that discovering the virus in the bloodstream of one out of one hundred and eleven blood tests was nothing more than an unexplained anomaly. But Dr. Horstmann's powerful scientific curiosity drove her to pursue the improbable as she considered why the polio virus was present in the blood. Was it possible that the virus in the little girl's blood might only be present for a short period of time?

She immediately left the hospital and returned to her Yale lab and conducted an experiment in which she fed a group of chimpanzees polio by the mouth to see if the virus turned up in the animals' blood. In a few days, the polio virus appeared in the chimps' bloodstreams, but the virus was only detectable for the brief period of time between incubation and before the chimps natural antibodies had formed to do their work.

While pursuing a peculiarity, Dr. Horstmann's lab tests on chimpanzees unearthed why Dr. Flexner, and all his researchers, had never detected the polio virus in the bloodstream. They had waited too long to take blood samples. Once the Rockefeller Institute declared that the polio virus had never appeared in the bloodstream, they created the foundation for all research opinions and ideas—for at least thirty years—until Dr. Horstmann made her discovery.

The best part of the Horstmann's story is that her scientific breakthrough opened the door toward the development of a vaccine.

Now researchers finally had two of the three puzzle pieces required to produce a successful vaccine. All that remained to solve the puzzle was to determine how to grow the polio virus in a safe medium, a process that had proved impossible because the only medium available to grow the virus had been the dangerous neurotropic medium produced by Flexner's MV viral strain.

However, in 1947, at the Research Division of Infectious Disease at the Children's Hospital of Boston, a scientist named John Franklin Enders Ph.D. stepped up to solve the four-decade-old polio virus conundrum.

John Enders was a twentieth century renaissance man. He attended Yale University, but in 1917, he left his studies to become a pilot in the U.S. Air Force. After the First World War ended, he returned to Yale where he was awarded a degree in 1920.

Initially, he chose a career in real estate but quickly became dissatisfied and entered Harvard University where he studied English Literature and the Germanic and Celtic languages with the idea of becoming a teacher of English, but again he was unhappy.

For much of his life, Enders had also entertained an interest in biology, and he decided to become a candidate for a Ph.D. degree in bacteriology and immunology. In 1930 he received his Ph.D.

Enders taught at Harvard until 1946, when he was asked to establish a laboratory for research into infectious diseases at the Children's Medical Center at Boston. Over a three year period, from1948 to 1950, with the assistance of his two young colleagues, Frederick C. Robbins, and Thomas H. Weller, he was able to grow the polio virus in various types of tissue, including non-nervous tissue. That discovery was the final piece to the polio vaccine puzzle—the major breakthrough that would allow labs to cultivate the huge quantities of the polio virus required to produce a successful vaccine.

In 1954, John F. Enders, Thomas H. Weller, and Fredrick C. Robbins were awarded the Nobel Prize in Physiology or Medicine—for their discovery of the ability of poliomyelitis viruses to grow in cultures of various types of tissue.

By today's standards, many of those we interviewed had hospital stays of incredibly long duration. Several recalled being hospitalized for nearly a year.
***Polio's Legacy: An Oral History,* Edmund Sass, ED. D.**

CHAPTER EIGHT

Summer 1945—Age 7—First Surgery
I'm seven now.
Mom still drives me to the clinic three times a week for physical therapy.
I go to the clinic a lot but I still can't walk without my brace.
I still can't stand unless mommy holds onto me.
A nurse tells me to sit on a table and lift my left foot up.
I try real hard but I can't.
A nurse holds my hand so I can walk.
I try to walk but my foot goes slap, slap, slap.
A nurse puts my brace on and tells me I can walk.
It's really hard to walk right.
With my brace I can walk okay but I can't run fast like my little brother.
The nurse gives me a rubber ball to squeeze on.

My hand is better but not as good as my other hand.
My daddy's in the army and we don't know where he is.
One morning my mom puts my PJs and my toothbrush into a paper bag and we drive downtown.
Uncle Bruce and Aunt Myrtle take my sister and brother to their house so Patty and Dicky can play with Donna and Clara.
Mom tells me that she waited for the summer vacation for my operation 'cause Doctor Lowman didn't want me to miss too much school.
I don't like school 'cause I miss a lot.
The hospital is close to the clinic where I go for physical therapy.
Mom parks the car.
We walk into the big building I start to cry 'cause she's going to leave me there.
A nurse walks up and takes my hand.
Mom hands the nurse the paper bag.
The nurse takes out my toothbrush.
Mom asks her about my PJ's.
The nurse tells her that I can't wear my PJ's.
Mom gives me a big kiss and a hug.
The nurse takes me to big door and pushes a button.
I am big now and don't cry but I can't stop sniffing.
The door opens and we walk in a little

room.
I remember daddy telling me to be brave.
The door closes and the floor moves.
The door opens and we walk.
With my brace on I can walk pretty good but not as fast as the nurse.
We walk past a big room filled with big round noisy metal things.
At the end of each metal thing there's a person's head sticking out.
Before the nurse pulls me away a little girl whose head is sticking out smiles.
I ask the nurse what those noisy metal things are.
She tells me they are called iron lungs and that room is the iron lung ward.
I start to cry and ask her if she is going to put me inside one of those things.
She says no. She says I'm a very lucky boy 'cause I'm just here for an operation.
We walk down the hall, through a door, and into a big room with lots of beds and boys.
By the door is a boy inside a baby crib.
I hope they're not going to put me in a baby crib.
The boy is standing and pulls on the sides of the crib.
He tries to talk but real words don't come out and he spits all over the floor.
I ask the nurse what is wrong with him.
She tells me he has cerebral palsy.

I ask her if that's like polio.
She shakes her head and says that cerebral palsy is a lot worse than polio.
We walk past the spitting boy and into the big room.
The nurse walks me to an empty bed and lifts me up.
On one side of my bed are four beds and on the other side are two. Across the room I count seven beds and those beds are next to a window.
The nurse takes my brace off and tells me that the boy in the bed on one side is named Juan, and the boy on the other side is Barry.
She hands me a funny shirt thing and tells me to stand up and put it on.
I try to stand up but without my brace I can't.
The nurse holds me and pushes my arms through some holes, turns me around and ties some strings together.
Then the nurse yells, "Boys, visiting hours start in fifteen minutes. Take care of any BMs or you will have to hold it for two hours."
The nurse starts to leave but she has my brace.
I ask her to give it back.
She tells me that I won't need it for a couple of months. She'll give it to my mom when she comes during visiting hours.

I ask Juan what is a BM?
He tells me that BM means a number two and asks me if my operation is tomorrow.
I tell him yes.
Juan tells me that if I don't get back from my operation in time, I'll miss the comic book man.
Barry tells me that he will let me read some of his comics if I get back too late.
I ask him who is the comic book man?
Barry tells me that every Monday, a man brings us a big box filled with new comic books. He stops at each bed and a boy can pick ten comic books. Then the man goes to the next bed and that boy can take ten comic books.
Barry tells me our ward has fourteen beds, plus the Spaz, so by the time the comic book man leaves we'll have about a thousand comic books.
Juan says that's a lot of comic books.
I ask Barry what is the Spaz?
He tells me the Spaz is the kid in the crib who spits on the floor.
A nurse walks in and tells us that it is time for visiting hours. A minute later my mom walks in and gives me a hug.
She looks around and sees my bed isn't by the window.
She tells me I'm on the wrong side of the room 'cause next week she is going to bring my sister and brother to the hospital. They

can't come inside the hospital but they can stand on the grass outside and wave. She says, she'll ask the nurse to move me to the window side so I can see my brother and sister wave back.

I tell her the nurse took my brace.

She tells me that's okay. By the time I'll be ready for my brace my shoe will be too small. So after I get back home, she'll have to buy me a new pair of shoes and she hopes the old brace still fits.

A nurse tells Mom that visiting hours are over. Mom hugs me and tells me that she'll see me tomorrow after the operation.

After the last visitor leaves, two nurses walk up and close the curtain around my bed. One nurse holds a tray with something that is covered with a towel. The other nurse tells me they have to give me something she calls an enema before my operation tomorrow.

The nurse sticks a black thing in my bottom.

I scream 'cause I don't like that.

After the lights go out most of the boys go to sleep.

I hear the bells ring from that church.

I wake up when a nurse lifts me off my bed and onto a bed that rolls.

I'm still sleepy when the nurse pushes me into a big room with a big bright light on the ceiling. Dr. Lowman pulls his white

mask off his face and smiles.
I try to smile back but a black, rubbery thing covers my mouth.
Then I wake up.
Mom is there.
I throw up.
I try to tell her that I want to go home, and my leg hurts, but I throw up again.

Dad or no dad, the day of my first operation eventually arrived, so my mom asked her mother, my Grandma Bardeen, to join her while she waited for me to recover from surgery.

Prior to the surgery, Dr. Lowman had explained to mom that he was going to start with what he called the least invasive surgery on me, though if the first try didn't correct the problem he'd have to try again with a second surgery. His goal was to do the least damage to my foot and ankle while still correcting my drop foot. It turned out that this strategy took three operations before most of my drop foot condition was corrected.

The morning of the surgery, mom was a little late picking up her mother, and to her surprise, her sister Teresa was also waiting there. When mom, Grandma Bardeen, and Aunt Teresa arrived at the hospital, a nurse told them the operation was over and I was already in the recovery room.

Mom long remembered that first moment

when she saw me. She said that my freckled face was pale and she had to fight to hold back her tears. She lifted the sheet by my feet and saw my left leg and foot were incased inside a white plaster cast that ran from my foot to my knee. The nurse told mom to sit down and wait for me to wake up from the anesthetic. Then the nurse warned mom that when I woke up, I would most likely vomit.

After a few minutes, mom saw my eyelids flutter and open. And then I did throw up, all over myself.

The nurse took off my dirty gown and put on a clean one.

I tried to sit up and threw up again.

While mom and the nurse changed me a second time, mom asked me if I had talked to Dr. Lowman before I went to sleep.

I told her that I did but I didn't remember what he said and that my leg hurt really bad.

Mom took my hand and reminded me that Dr. Lowman had told me my leg would hurt for a while, but I would feel better soon. Then she said that Dr. Lowman had told her that during this first operation he would only transplant one muscle, hoping that it might help me lift my left foot. If not, I had more muscles he could transplant during future operations. What she didn't say was how dearly she hoped that the first operation would be the last one.

Mom got angry when an orderly walked into the recovery room pushing a gurney. The nurse told mom that it was time for me to return to the boys' ward.

She grabbed me and told the nurse that we'd barely had time to talk.

The nurse told her that mom and her relatives could return in five days, during regular visiting hours. Then the nurse reminded mom that children under the age of eighteen were not allowed inside the hospital to visit patients.

Mom remembered trying to kiss me, but the orderly pushed my gurney past her and into the hall.

Recently, as I gazed at old photos of the original Orthopedic Hospital, I was amazed to see how nice the building looked and to discover the place was not the grim edifice I recalled. The three-story Spanish style structure was nearly a block long and had a red tile roof and landscaped grounds. In those photographs, the hospital looked like an inviting place, so why did I burst into tears the moment I entered the building that morning of my first surgery? That's an easy guess. My seven-and-a-half-year-old nose had picked up the acrid aroma of antiseptic and the memories of those endless, terrible days in the Communicable Disease Building at the County Hospital returned. I reacted like a family pet that suddenly realizes it is being dragged into the veterinarian's office.

As the nurse walked me down a long hall toward the boys' ward, she probably tried to shield me from looking into the iron lung ward, but she wasn't quick enough, and that young girl's sweet, but sad smile, remains etched in my memory to this day.

All day the nursing staff hovered around the boys' ward, but completing their daily tasks seemed more important than getting to know the boys. The night orderly was the only person in the hospital who took the time to converse with us. A few weeks after my surgery, the night orderly told me that because iron lung patients could not breathe outside the device, all the orderlies did whatever they could to keep from being assigned to the iron lung ward.

At the time, I didn't understand exactly what he meant, but much later, as I did research for this book, I discovered that caring for the daily needs of an iron lung patient was the most intensive work at the Orthopedic Hospital.

Iron lung patients had to be fed by hand three times a day.

The bedding and clothing had to be changed at least daily and more as required.

All iron lung patients, be they child or adult, wore diapers, and those diapers had to be changed as needed.

Finally, all iron lung patients had to be turned on a regular basis to avoid bedsores. To the orderly, an iron lung ward assignment meant working with patients who could die while you changed their diaper.

Another sad memory from that first summer surgery was the drooling, spitting boy in the crib. My next bed neighbor, Barry, taught me to use that derogatory term, Spaz. Today, I am ashamed to admit that during all four of my hospital stays I called the spitting boy trapped in the crib by that nickname. Back in those days, most of America's kids called people with cerebral palsy spastic, or spaz. In fact, the majority of Jerry Lewis' comedy act was based on a man who couldn't control his arms, legs, or his mouth.

Now, how big was the boys' ward and what did it look like? The ward, my home for six weeks after the first operation, was a rectangular room approximately forty-five by twenty-five feet with tall windows on the exterior wall that faced west. Seven of the fourteen beds were under the windows and the other half were against the interior, or east wall. The walls were painted a light green and the floors were a darker green linoleum. There were no pictures on the walls. No drapes, or curtains on the windows. In fact, there was nothing about the boys' ward that could be considered in anyway decorative, or stylish. The beds were made out of metal and were adjustable, as long as the patient could get out of bed and turn the handle at the foot of the bed. It didn't take me long to figure out that the nurses were always too busy to spend any of their valuable time cranking my bed up or down.

During my first surgery my bed was on the interior wall in the middle of the room. To the right of each bed there was a small nightstand. On the top of the nightstand sat a metal pitcher full of water and a glass made out of real glass, not plastic (this was 1945 after all). Below the pitcher of water there was a single drawer for my toothbrush, but the toothbrush drawer was also where most of the boys stashed their comic books. Below the drawer there were two shelves. The first shelf housed my urinal, and the lower shelf was for my bedpan.

When the nurse took my brace from me, the reason I panicked was that it had taken me months and months of hard, painful work to learn to how walk again. Although I didn't know it at the time, after each operation to correct my drop foot, I would have to go through learning how to walk all over again.

Barry's prediction that I would miss the comic book man that first Monday was correct, but by the time the comic man came around the week following my surgery, I was ready for him.

Every Monday each boy could select ten comic books out of the big metal bin. By the time twenty-four hours had passed, we'd all read all ten comics and each of us would hand his ten comic books to the boy in the next bed. Come Friday, every boy in the ward, except for the Spaz, had memorized each picture, and read every word from the one hundred and forty comic books.

Why were we so enamored with the comics? It is simple. In 1945 the boys in the third floor ward had nothing to do except read comic books. The ward had no television sets or radios. Also, this was summertime and fourteen boys, ages five to eleven, were trapped in their beds for weeks or even months. Their normal way of burning off their unbounded energy, running around the neighborhood with their brother or friends, had been taken away. At least reading comic books gave us something to do.

But comic books were but one of the two major subjects in every boy's daily conversation. The other topic? Bowel movements.

All nurses in the ward seemed to be obsessed with the bowel movements of every boy. At the end of each bed was a chart, and among items monitored, the record tracked the time of day a bed pan was used, and a complete description of the bed pan contents.

In the morning when the head nurse made her rounds through the ward, she would stop at each bed and review every chart. If a boy went a day without a BM, the head nurse would say, "Charlie, I see you didn't have a BM yesterday.

You know what that means. After breakfast, you'll be given a pill. If that doesn't solve the problem, tomorrow you'll will be given an enema."

The boys called those pills Brown Bombers, and when, for instance, Charlie received his pill all the boys chanted, "Swallow that Brown Bomber and go, Charlie, go."

You might get the impression that the nurses at the Orthopedic Hospital were not very friendly, and to some extent that is correct. In fact, over my four long hospital stays, the nurses never came across as a best buddy. But that was because they had one of the toughest jobs in the world. Those women worked round the clock trying to prevent all the young boys from getting infections after their surgeries.

Did I dislike all the nurses? Not really, although as a group, the orderlies were friendlier. While mopping the floors they would come by our beds, stop pushing the mop for a moment or two, and sometimes they'd talk to us, or answer a question. To the best of my recollection, a nurse never had time to do that. So there you have a quick snapshot of life in the third floor boys' ward at the Orthopedic Hospital during the six weeks of my 1945 summer.

Sister Kenny's approach was totally contrary to the accepted medical treatment of the time which typically involved long-term splinting and plaster body casts to immobilize the limbs, combined with prolonged bed rest. Unfortunately for the many who received it, this standard practice of immobilization did more harm than good, causing atrophy and inflexibility in already weakened limbs.
***Polio's Legacy: An Oral History,* Edmund Sass, ED. D.**

CHAPTER NINE

Nurses: The Heroic, The Brave, And The Indifferent

As I collected stories, histories, and family recollections for this memoir, I ultimately came to the conclusion that the successful outcome of my eleven-year journey depended on two women of courage.

The first was my mom, who decided early on that she would allow nothing, and that included her marriage, to get in the way of my complete recovery.

The other woman of courage was a self-taught "bush" nurse from the outback of Australia named Elizabeth Kenny. Her life story is one of self-initiative, true grit, and a stubborn streak that would put Winston

Churchill to shame.

Elizabeth Kenny was born in1880 in Warialda, New South Wales, Australia.

At age seventeen, she broke her wrist when she fell from a horse. Her father took her to Dr. Aeneas McDonnell in Toowoomba where she remained during her convalescence. While there, she studied McDonnell's anatomy books. After her wrist bone healed, she spent her next seven years working as an unaccredited nurse in the wild Australian outback, also called the bush.

In 1909, at the age of twenty-nine, she assumed the role of an official nurse after paying a tailor to make her a nurse's uniform, complete with an official cap and cape.

During the following years she encountered her first cases of childhood polio while working in the bush. Observing that the polio patients' muscles were locked, she applied hot compresses made from woolen blankets to the affected limbs. To everyone's surprise, several afflicted children recovered with no serious after-effects.

When World War One began, she volunteered to serve as a nurse for wounded military personnel. She still had not received any formal training but nurses were badly needed, so she was accepted and assigned to a "dark ship"—a large transport vessel that ran during the night with all lights off between Australia and England, carrying war goods and soldiers. On the return voyage to Australia, her ship carried wounded soldiers and trade goods. She served on these dangerous missions throughout the war, making sixteen round trips and one voyage completely around the world via the Panama Canal.

In 1917, she was accorded the title "Sister", a rank in the Australian Army Nurse Corps that is the equivalent of a first lieutenant. She continued to use the title for the rest of her life.

After the war, Sister Kenny returned to Australia to care for her niece, Maude, who had been disabled with polio.

Sister Kenny recalled her early success using hot wool blankets to treat polio patients in the Australian outback, and she used that same method with her niece. After eighteen months under Sister Kenny's method of hot packs and muscle stretching, Maude was able to walk again. Maude returned to Townsville, married, and conceived a child. The newspapers in Townsville took up Maude's story, publicizing her recovery from polio as a cure.

In 1932, Queensland suffered its worst polio epidemic in thirty years resulting in hundreds of sick and paralyzed children. During that epidemic, Sister Kenny used her hot pack protocol on as many children as she could, and the following year, several local people helped her set up a rudimentary polio-treatment facility under canopies outside the Queens Hotel in Townsville. In a few months, after proving her success with local children, she moved her facility into the first floor of the hotel. The first official medical evaluation of Sister Kenny's protocol on patients who were struggling to recover after quarantine took place in Townsville in 1934, under the auspices of the Queensland Health Department. The evaluation of her work led to the establishment of Sister Kenny polio clinics in several cities in Australia.

During the late thirties, Sister Kenny refined her clinical method and made a formal request to the Queensland Health Department that she be permitted to run a clinical trial on patients during the acute stages of polio. She hoped to prove that her protocol was better than the standard accepted immobilization method, but the Australian medical establishment would not allow her to treat patients until after the acute stage of the disease, or until muscle tightness or cramping had already subsided.

Throughout the world, in the 1920s and 1930s, the standard medical procedure for dealing with polio patients still consisted of immobilizing their affected limbs with a Bradford Frame, splints, or plaster casts. In 1939, the NFIP stockpiled 15,000 Bradford Frames and Toronto splints in New York City, to be ready for shipment wherever U. S. doctors required them to show the medical establishments belief in immobilization.

Why would the medical professionals refuse Sister Kenny's request for a clinical trial? I can only assume that they did not want to be told how to practice medicine by a woman who was not an MD, and in fact, lacked any type of formal medical education.

Rejected by the established medical professionals in Australia, Sister Kenny ignored their refusal for a clinical trial, and used her hot packs on a single polio patient at the George Street Clinic in Brisbane during the acute stage of the illness.

Weeks later, Sister Kenny's patient recovered with fewer after-effects than those experienced by patients placed in plaster casts or braces. This proved, even to the orthodox Australian medical establishment, that the Sister Kenny method was far superior to the immobilization treatment.

At last recognized in her home country, the New South Wales government paid for Sister Kenny's passage across the Pacific Ocean to present her radical polio clinical method to American medical professionals.

Just how radical were her techniques?

At the time, the medical establishment thought that after a muscle had lost its strength or had been paralyzed, it could not be retrained and that the loss of strength was irretrievable, but Sister Kenny relaxed the effected limb, or limbs with heat and then stretched it, revitalizing the muscles through massage with the goal that the patient would regain some, if not all control of the muscles in the effected limbs.

Sister Kenny's ship docked in Los Angeles. She presented her findings to medical professionals in Southern California, and then in San Francisco, Chicago, New York City, and the Mayo Clinic.

At first, the success of Sister Kenny's method in Australia was ignored by American medical professionals, but before her planned return to Australia, she was offered the opportunity to demonstrate her work to Doctors Miland Knapp and John Pohl, who headed the polio treatment center in Minneapolis, Minnesota. They had reviewed Sister Kenny's Australian successes and they invited her to remain in Minneapolis to demonstrate her methods on the polio patients there.

Dr. Knapp and Dr. Pohl immediately recognized the success of the Kenny method and they asked her to stay.

Two years later, the Sister Kenny Institute was established. Her pioneering principles of muscle rehabilitation became the foundation of modern physical therapy. For the next eleven years, Minneapolis became Sister Kenny's base in America and during that time, hundreds of doctors attended her classes at the University of Minnesota to learn her radical techniques.

As a result, Sister Kenny treatment centers were opened throughout the United States. She received honorary degrees from Rutgers University and the University of Rochester, lunched with President Roosevelt, and, in 1952, was ranked by a Gallup Poll as America's most admired woman.

I owe the fact that I was never strapped into a Bradford Frame or incased in plaster casts, and the fact that my muscles were consequently in reasonable shape for my multiple operations, to the tenacity of this heroic woman. Had Sister Elizabeth Kenny given up in Chicago and returned to Australia, Dr. Lowman would have never been able to predict, or produce my eventual success.

Even after Sister Kenny's treatment was proven to be the best for the patient, she continued to do morning rounds in hospitals where she was known to cut off immobilization splints, and remove braces that had been ordered by the male-dominated medical establishment during her absence. So for the thousands, including me, who became infected with the polio virus after 1942, we applaud her stubbornness and unwillingness to back down in the face of overwhelming odds.

As I wrote the words in the previous paragraph, I had a fuzzy memory of meeting Sister Kenny during one of my hospital stays. After much thought and investigation, I have come to the conclusion that in 1947, during my second operation, I joined many polio patients in the hospital auditorium where we watched the 1946 movie, Sister Kenny. After the movie was over, before I was wheeled back to the third floor boys' ward, I shook the hand of Rosalind Russell, the actress who portrayed Sister Kenny in the film. To be honest, I never actually met Sister Kenny, but I did talk with Rosalind Russell, and that's not bad for a nine-year-old kid who still couldn't walk three steps without his brace.

This eternally grateful polio survivor knows that Sister Elizabeth Kenny changed my destiny and the futures of thousands of polio survivors. That's a lot to say for a self-taught nurse from the Australian outback, but what about the rest of those nurses—the brave and the indifferent?

In reality, nurses are the glue that holds the medical profession together. Unlike most doctors, they have the only daily, face-to-face contact with the patients they serve, and risk their lives in the process, such as the worldwide Ebola crisis of 2014, during which two nurses from the U. S. became infected with the very disease they were attempting to treat.

If working in an environment that could make you ill, or die, constitutes bravery, then the nurses who worked throughout the United States during the decades of polio were certainly brave individuals. I repeat this harrowing statistic from the records of the Los Angeles County Hospital: In the late 1930s, more than a hundred nurses were paralyzed and never again worked in a professional capacity due to being infected during the polio epidemics.

Polio does not recognize civic, state, or international borders. Canada reported its worst epidemic in 1953 when verified polio cases reached 60 per 100,000 of the population. That rate of infection was the highest in North America, and among the highest in the world.

A Canadian nurse recounted her first day on the job during the 1953 epidemic year. She was assigned to a ward with twelve patients in iron lungs. After a quick tour of the room, she realized that she actually knew three of the patients. Before her shift ended, she was stunned to learn that all three had died.

So between Sister Kenny, the two nurses infected with Ebola, the one hundred and ten

Los Angeles nurses permanently disabled by polio in the 1930s, or the Canadian nurse who watched members of her community suffer and die, how could I possibly suggest that some nurses seemed indifferent?

Let us take the example of polio patients who lived their lives inside iron lungs. Those patient were totally dependent on a staff of nurses to meet all of their physical needs to change their soiled diapers, to feed them, to scratch their nose, renew their bedding, and to even turn the pages of the book they read.

To care for a completely paralyzed iron lung patient was so labor intensive that the nurses were required to follow a strict routine. It didn't take long for helpless iron lung patients to learn that they had to fit their needs into the nurses' routine, or their lives, such as they were, could become even more hellish.

The "follow the nurses' routine" concept affected all patients in a hospital, not just the iron lung ward, and that included me, a young kid who still had a lot to learn. But I quickly figured out that holding my breath or otherwise displaying anger at a nurse was not going to work in my favor. Early on I learned to adopt the role of the good patient, and to work with, not against, the daily routine of the nursing staff. I was not fully paralyzed or in an iron lung, but as my left leg was in a cast and I could not get out of bed, I was totally dependent on the staff of nurses who were responsible for the third floor boys' ward to take away my smelly bedpan, to refill my water bottle, or to bring me a pill to mask the pain during the night.

During my long recoveries in the hospital I witnessed some slow response times to a patient in need, but it seemed to me that the slow responses always happened to the most troublesome patients.

Most nurses were dedicated professionals who attempted to complete twelve hours worth of tasks in an eight hour shift, but all nurses did not fit that description. While researching for this book, I read of one case where a nurse threatened to shut off a girl's iron lung if she didn't stop crying. The girl continued to cry. The nurse turned off the respirator, and the girl immediately passed out. The girl's parents found out and had that nurse removed from the iron lung ward, but as far as I could determine, that nurse continued to work at the same hospital, just on a different floor in a different ward.

Nurses who worked in the iron lung ward had to force themselves to become less compassionate. Even the most forthright nurses would agree that they were overwhelmed by the iron lung patient's needs and that the nursing staff never felt they were allotted enough time to complete all of their duties. Some of those nurses who didn't have enough time to process their stress and grief would shut down their feelings, a form of Post Traumatic Stress Disorder (PTSD).

Imagine for a moment that you are a patient who cannot move a muscle below your neck. You are lying in your own feces and have been that way for some time. You call for a nurse. She, or he, has to temporarily slide you out of the iron lung to clean up your mess. To you, an iron lung patient, each moment spent outside your metal cocoon is life threatening. You panic and fight back in the only way you have, by crying, pleading, screaming, or cursing. The attending nurse has two choices: Endure your angry tirades and complete the job, or slide you back inside and let you lie in your filth until the next shift takes over.

In my opinion, the majority of the tales of nursing indifference during the polio era were the result of patient fear and an over-worked staff. Luckily, indifferent nurses were not the norm and all but one of the nurses I encountered during my four extended hospital stays were competent, friendly, and caring. I will detail the story of my indifferent nurse in a future chapter.

Recently, after sixty-five years of outstanding health, I came down with a lymphoma blood cancer that nearly killed me. The experience wasn't fun, but my brush with cancer gave me the opportunity to get up close and personal with today's nurses and all of the modern-day professionals I encountered in the infusion room earned my complete and total respect.

On my first day in the infusion room, where I was to receive my initial treatment of Rituxan, a lifesaving monoclonal antibody that would seek out and kill off my blood cancer, memories of my first operation filled my thoughts. I knew that it took every member of my polio team, Doctor Lowman, and the whole staff of the Orthopedic Hospital, to give me back my ability to stand straight and walk like a man.

And as the liter of Rituxan dripped, drop by drop, into my veins, I glanced around the infusion room and watched a staff of medical professionals treat all of their patients with care and respect. I realized that I was now a member of a new medical team—my oncologist, Doctor Ye, and the infusion room staff—a single-minded group of medical professionals who were dedicated to killing off the lymphoma cancer cells that filled my bone marrow before the cancer killed me.

Cindy Wilson, an RN who works in the Oncology Infusion Room, told me, "I really hit my stride as a nurse when I transferred to the infusion room staff, because cancer patients really get it. They understand, and the nurses understand, what's at stake, and that relationship allows us to become very close. When any of our patients die, we all mourn. Sometimes it is difficult to find the time to weep, so on a regular basis, the nursing staff will close the infusion room thirty minutes early and the hospital chaplain will join us to assist as we work through our grief." Today, hospital staffs understand that the overwhelming emotional loads carried by nurses, must themselves be treated. Otherwise, like soldiers on the front lines of battle, they will eventually shut down their feelings and slip into PTSD. As a grown man who "forgot" my childhood polio experiences until my grandchildren asked the questions that inspired this book, I understand.

As I write this story, I have been in remission for over two years, and, as the infusion room nurses have reminded me many times, when a future medical problem arises, I am to call the infusion room first, explain my problem, and let the nurse who answers the phone tell me what I should do next.

If Sister Elizabeth Kenny were alive today, I think she would agree with my impression of the infusion room nursing staff by exclaiming, "Mate, those infusion room nurses are brilliant!"

In the nation's capital, crowds danced on the lawn of the White House and chanted, "We want Harry." Finally, President Harry S Truman stepped out and proclaimed, "This is the day we have been waiting for since Pearl Harbor. This is the day when Fascism finally dies, as we always knew it would."
http://www.historynet.com/v-j-day-1945-the-world-rejoices.htm

CHAPTER TEN

The Dalton's are Moving, Moving and Moving

While World War Two was grinding to a halt there was a lot happening to the Dalton family.

As soon as Germany surrendered in May, 1945, mom hoped that my dad would quickly come home from the army. Once or twice a week we'd get a letter from him. Mom would read them to us, but he never told us where he was, so mom guessed that he must be somewhere in the Pacific fighting the Japanese.

She dearly wanted my dad to come home and go back to work at the post office. Between raising three children, my polio, the extra cost of gas for the trips to physical therapy sessions, and my expensive shoes and brace, mom was having real trouble making ends meet on his army pay.

I do not know if the lack of money was the

reason, but during the years my dad was in the army we moved a lot. The first move was to a house in Beverly Hills where Emmy, my mom's sister-in-law, lived with her young son. My mom's brother, Hugh Bardeen, had been killed during an Air Force training flight in Texas and what she told us was that we moved to help Emmy get through the shock of her husband's death.

Emmy was a nice lady, and we had fun playing with her son, little Hugh. My most vivid memory of those days happened when another of my mom's brothers, Knox, stopped by to see if mom wanted to go to the UCLA/USC football game at the Los Angeles Coliseum. She told Knox no. He jumped into his car and I watched him drive down the block. Suddenly the car stopped, and reversed back to Aunt Emmy's house. Knox jumped out of his car and asked my mom if I could come with him. This time she said yes, and I went with my uncle Knox to the biggest football game of the year. Every seat was filled and I joined with more than one hundred thousand cheering football fans. On either side of the Los Angeles Coliseum sat the UCLA and USC fans including large sections where spectators sat and held special cards. The cards were turned and flipped to produce huge pictures. The colorful UCLA and USC marching bands paraded up and down the field, and there were deafening roars from the UCLA or USC fans each time a touchdown was scored.

When I was grown, I came to know that in the view of most of the Bardeen family, my Uncle Knox had achieved less out of his life than they thought he should have. But in my view, he took the time to think of his nephew, and that simple act of kindness gave me one of the most memorable days of my childhood.

We moved a second time some months later, this time to a house in Burbank so we could live closer to my mom's older sister, Ester Marshall, and her family.

Finally, we move into Grandma and Grandpa Dalton's home on Orange Grove Avenue, about a mile west of the home where we had lived when I caught polio. We stayed there, waiting for our dad to come back from the war, living with a grandma who never smiled and a grandpa who spent most of his time in his backyard garden planting seeds. The contrast between the two grandparents was striking. Grandpa Dalton was quiet and gentle. He would take my sister, my brother, and me into his lath house in the backyard and explain to us how he hybridized roses, show us how to turn over a compost pile, and teach us the proper time to plant flower seeds.

On the other hand, Grandma Dalton was neither quiet nor gentle. She would wake up with the sun, boil water on the stove, and then dip a piece of dry toast into the scalding water and without bothering to put in her set of false teeth, gum the soggy bread into submission. She pretty much told all of us, and that included my mom, what to do and when to do it.

One day, I saw grandma use a jelly glass to measure the amount of bleach, and then dump the bleach into the washing machine. From that moment, I never drank water, juice, or anything out of my grandma's jelly glasses.

I cannot help but wonder why Grandpa and Grandma Dalton married. Grandpa grew up in Los Angeles, while grandma was born in Minnesota. When we lived together I was only a boy of seven or eight, but Grandma and Grandpa Dalton looked to me like the opposite ends of a magnet.

Mom later admitted that she was not happy having to live with Grandma and Grandpa Dalton, but our family financial situation required it. Things got so tight that a friend from our church helped mom get a job chopping cabbage to make coleslaw at a fish restaurant inside the famous Farmer's Market on Fairfax.

The days mom worked, she would walk the three blocks to Pico. There she would catch the bus at the corner of Pico and Fairfax and ride five miles north to the Farmer's Market. I'm sure that she rode the bus to save our rationed gas for my my physical therapy session drives downtown. After the war was over and my dad had returned home, to the best of my knowledge, my mom never stepped on a public bus or streetcar again.

Before the war ended, my life pretty much consisted of going to school, visits to physical therapy, and trips to the brace shop. But after VJ day in September of 1945, we got a letter from my dad telling us that he had left the Philippines on a ship and he was heading home. After a long boat ride across the Pacific Ocean, he finally returned to Los Angeles when it was nearly Christmas. He told us he had a four week leave and then he was going to be stationed at an historic army base called Fort Warren in Cheyenne, Wyoming.

Much later, my sister confided to me that our mom told her that she was very pleased with the news because she wanted our father to stay in the army. He was an officer, a position she felt carried more prestige than a lowly postman.

But my mom's hope for a husband who was an officer and a gentleman, rather than a postal clerk, ran head-on into the reality of Congress and the American people, who were worn out after four years of war. At the end of the largest conflict in human history, there were more than eight million American soldiers in uniform. Two years later, the army consisted of 700,000 troops and the remaining army officers who had any thought of advancing through the ranks all had graduated from West Point, not Santa Monica Junior College.

Regardless of the impending reduction of armed forces, my dad left for Cheyenne just after Christmas.

Before we left Los Angeles, my mom checked with Doctor Lowman to let him know we were going to Cheyenne, Wyoming, and she'd make an appointment if and when we returned.

Worried over the capability of our pre-war Studebaker to make the nearly 1200 mile trip, not comfortable with driving in winter conditions, and the expenses involved with the car trip, it took mom until June to build up the required funds and the confidence. In spite of her concerns, we left Grandpa and Grandma's house with our pre-war car loaded up with three kids and nearly all of our belongings. We joined our dad in Cheyenne five days later and the family didn't return to Los Angeles until the fall of 1947.

Fort Warren had been built in 1867 and was originally named Fort D. A. Russell. In 1930, the name of the base was changed to Fort Francis E. Warren honoring Wyoming's territorial governor and first state governor. Not long after we left Cheyenne, the installation became an Air Force base, and by 1960, Warren AFB was a fully operational

Intercontinental Ballistic Missile site.

To an eight-year-old boy from the "big city" of Los Angeles, the open country around Cheyenne was an endless playground with warm summer days.

My family was together for the first time since 1943 and during that year my brother and I had a great time. We explored the countryside, we fished for trout, we marched like real soldiers on the historic parade field, and we saluted our dad each time he strapped on a Colt 45 as required for the Officer of the Day.

All three of us kids attended elementary school in Cheyenne and for children born and raised in Los Angeles, we were shocked and excited to wake up on the first day of school to see that snow had fallen during the night and covered the ground.

A school bus from town picked up all the army kids to take them to school in Cheyenne. I will never forget running across the front yard to the school bus that first day. All three Dalton children fell face down onto the white snow in front of the school bus filled with children. We fell because the thick blanket of white had hidden the drop-off between the curb and the street. Cold, wet, and red-faced was not the best way to meet our new fellow students.

The school was okay, but on the first day,

my third grade teacher asked me to write my name and the city I came from on the blackboard using cursive script. I told her that at my school in Los Angeles, we were going to learn cursive script in the third grade. She told me she was sorry, but in Wyoming students were taught cursive script in the second grade so I should go ahead and do the best I could.

That's why my handwriting is so poor, or at least my excuse and I'm sticking to it no matter what.

Years later, when my sister and I reminisced about our days in Cheyenne, she claimed she had noticed some subtle changes in the relationship between our parents. Pat was two years older than I was so perhaps she did.

Prior to the war, nearly all married women were housewives. But from the day the bombs dropped on Pearl Harbor, the women of America took on the role of "Rosie the Riveter" in factories, or became the heads of their households at home.

And added to our mom's new responsibilities was a son with a brace that absorbed more than his share of our families assets and time.

After the war, all over America, women now realized that they were capable of most anything. The change in our parent's relationship that my sister had observed was not unique to our family.

After one of the snowiest and coldest winters on record, we left Cheyenne on May 3, 1947. I remember that date because our school had scheduled a May Day celebration and the festivities had to be cancelled due to a huge snow storm.

The army, in it's infinite wisdom, decided to discharge my father from the service by sending all of us across the country to Fort Eustis, which was located close to the Naval Weapons Station adjacent to Yorktown, Virginia.

I'm positive my mom felt that my dad had somehow let her and the family down when we moved into our new "living" quarters. The housing assigned to families whose fathers were being discharged was an old naval complex and consisted of rows of two-story buildings with four units per building. The structures had been painted a thin coat of Army olive drab over the Navy's battleship gray and the structures looked as if the last paint job had been applied before the war. During our first week there, we had no furniture beyond a mattress for each person, a stove, a refrigerator, and a table with two chairs so the adults could eat sitting down.

As far as I was concerned, except for the hot, sticky climate, the lack of furniture and sleeping on a mattress, it was like we were camping. There were lots of kids whose dads were being discharged, and we soon learned that after a short hike through a thick, jungle-like forest behind our house, we could play soldier in the trenches at the Yorktown National Historical Park. Our pretend battles would go on and on until one of the park rangers spotted us and chased us away.

While my dad was waiting to get out of the army, he ran the officers' club, which was similar to an exclusive country club at a private golf course.

The main thing I recall about the officers' club was that my dad would lift us up and show us where to drop a nickel into one of the slot machines. The really good part was he let us keep the winnings. One time I was a big winner when I won five whole nickels. Trust me, to a nine-year-old boy in the summer of 1947, twenty-five cents was big bucks!

After three summer months of fun in hot and humid Virginia, my dad finally received his discharge. Following a brief stop-over in Washington, D.C., we headed west—across the whole country—in our trusty pre-war Studebaker. Once we arrived in Los Angeles, we moved back into Grandma and Grandpa Dalton's home on Orange Grove, the last place we had lived while my dad was in the army.

Surgeries were often scheduled during the summer so that loss of school time would be minimized . . . In addition, many young polio survivors had multiple surgeries to treat their many deformities, or sometimes to redo or repair surgeries that had failed the first time.
Living With Polio: The Epidemic and its Survivors,
Daniel J. Wilson

CHAPTER FIVE

1947—SECOND SURGERY

After one operation I still can't lift my left foot. Dr. Lowman tells me this time he'll move a stronger muscle.
One Sunday, mom and dad drive me to the hospital.
This time's different 'cause I'm going to miss Christmas and lots of school.
I don't mind missing school but not Christmas!
Mom promises me that the Christmas tree will stay up, and my presents will stay under the tree 'til I get home.
Mom and dad stay with me until a nurse takes my hand and we walk to the elevator that takes us to the third floor.
As I walk down the hall, everything looks the same.
As we walk by the iron lung ward, I slow down but that little girl isn't there

anymore.
We pass the crib with the Spaz. He's still drooling, spitting, and tries to say something.
I ask, "How long has he been there?"
The nurse looks back, sort of like she forgot he's there. "I'm not sure. I've been here a little more than a year and he's been there all that time. Kenny, your bed's the empty one by the window."
Mom I'll be happy. I finally get a bed by the window. I crawl to the window, look out and see where my brother and sister will stand on the grass below.
The nurse lifts me onto the bed, takes my brace off and tells me they're going to give me an enema so I'll be ready for my operation the next morning.
I hate that, but I learned the last time that the nurses are the boss, so I just lay down and watch her close the curtain around my bed.
Later, I check out the other beds in the ward.
Barry's gone and so is Juan, so except for the Spaz, everyone's gone.
I don't know any of the other kids. Some of them are younger than me, some older, but they all look scared just like me.
After a really bad dinner of some kind of watery soup and Jello, the lights go out.
I hear a couple of kids start to cry, but I

don't cry 'cause I am nine, and I promised my dad that I am going to be brave.

I want to go to sleep but I can't stop thinking about that stinky black mask they put on my face before the last operation. I try to stop thinking about that and hope I don't dream about it tonight.

It is still dark when a nurse and an orderly lift me onto a gurney and push me down the long hall to the operating room.

Inside the room everything looks the same. The table. The giant light on the ceiling. The doctor holding the black mask. As the mask comes closer I try to twist my head away but a hand stops me. A man's voice tells me to take a deep breath. I do and the next thing I hear is my mom telling me to open my eyes.

I do and the room starts to spin.

Mom grabs a spit pan and gets it under my chin just in time. I don't throw up much 'cause they didn't give me any breakfast, but just like the last operation, I threw up something 'cause the walls are moving round and round.

Mom and dad give me a kiss and that's when I feel a giant pain in my left leg.

I try to sit up to see my leg, get real dizzy, and almost throw up again.

Mom pulls back the sheet and I see the white cast. This is bigger and longer than the first one.

I lay back down and sort of listen to mom and dad talk to me. Then an orderly takes me back to the ward.
All the boys are reading their new comic books. I remember that Monday morning is comic book day. But I'm too sleepy, and hurting to care about that.
I close my eyes and don't wake up until the nurse puts my dinner on the tray.
The next morning, Doctor Lowman with a bunch of other doctors stops by my bed.
Doctor Lowman lifts my cast up.
It hurts.
Dr. Lowman talks to the other doctors about the new muscle he transplanted.
Every morning, Doctor Lowman, and other doctors stop by my bed.
The head nurse calls it the morning rounds.
One of the nurse's rules is that all the boys have to finish breakfast, brush their teeth, and comb their hair before morning rounds start.
One day after my operation, when my leg isn't hurting so bad, a man walks up to my bed. He tells me he is going to cut a small hole in my cast, down by my ankle, so the doctors can see my scar. I ask him if it is going to hurt. He tells me no. I watch him plug in a little electric saw and he starts to cut into my cast at my ankle. After a few seconds, white stuff is flying, and my ankle

starts to get real hot.
I scream for a nurse. She runs up and holds my hand while the man finishes cutting the hole. After he leaves, I look at the cast by my ankle and I don't see any blood, but that saw really scares me.
The next Monday, the comic book man comes and I get my ten comic books. My favorite comics are Batman, Superman, and Captain Marvel 'cause I'm not a little kid anymore.
At the other end of the ward, over by the window, a nurse sets a little Christmas tree on a table. There are a few ornaments hanging on the tree but no presents.
One day a man and a woman walk into the ward, yell Merry Christmas, and give each boy a toy car and a piece of peppermint candy. The next day the same thing happens except this time we all get a stuffed bear. The next day another toy and some candy are passed out. It is like everyday is Christmas day for the boys on the third floor.
Then one day, a man comes in and gives each boy a squirt gun!
No boy says anything until the last nurse walks out of the ward. Then we all fill up our water guns and squirt each other as fast as we can.
I guess we make too much noise laughing and yelling 'cause the head nurse comes in

a takes all the squirt guns away.
I leave the hospital in January and my mom and dad take me home to a real Christmas tree. There are lots of presents with my name under the tree. Finally I rip the wrapping paper off the biggest box and there's a real Erector set complete with a wind-up motor.
This is my best Christmas ever!

While my parents, and grandparents were trying to figure out how we were all going to fit into Grandpa and Grandma Dalton's house, my mom made an appointment for me to see Doctor Lowman. He checked out my leg and saw that I still couldn't lift my foot. He looked into scheduling me for my second muscle transplant surgery, but it was too late in the year for him to program my operation during summer vacation. Instead, he scheduled the operation for early December, which meant I would be in the hospital over Christmas. He also determined that my old brace and shoe were over a year old, and either needed to be replaced or tossed, but he wanted to see the results of the second operation before deciding if I still needed to wear a brace. He also reminded mom that once I was able to walk without a brace, I would still require about a three-inch build-up on the heel of my left shoe. He assured mom that the three-inch difference would be corrected with my final surgery and within a year, after trimming down my built-up heel each month, I would end up with legs of equal length and walk with a normal gait.

Returning to the Orthopedic Hospital for my second operation was both good and bad for me. It was good because this time I knew what was going to happen, no surprises before, during, and after the operation. It was bad because I knew that along with the pain, being away from home for another six to eight weeks was going to be long and lonely. And the worst thing of all, I was going to miss opening my presents on Christmas morning.

But as I look back, my situation was nowhere as bad or as hopeless as the boy we all called the Spaz.

His bed was away from the rest of the beds, tucked into a little alcove that connected the boys' ward to the main hallway. Whenever someone came in or out of the ward, they had to pass by the Spaz.

He had a severe case of cerebral palsy and we all called him Spaz because he couldn't stop his hands, legs, shoulders, and head from making awkward, jerky movements. He couldn't talk or do anything beyond standing or sitting on his bed with his arms and legs flailing around.

And when the Spaz tried to talk, his mouth would contort, his lips would twitch, and he'd spit or slobber all over anyone who got too close.

One Monday, a new orderly made a terrible mistake. He told the comic book man to give the Spaz ten comic books. The kid tore the pages and drooled all over the comics so bad that none of the rest of us wanted to touch them. The boys in the ward made sure that the new orderly saw what the Spaz did to the comics, and the next Monday, the orderly told the comic book man to skip the Spaz during the handout. That worked for a while until we had to train another new orderly.

As I did the research for this book, I learned that cerebral palsy could be loosely translated as 'brain paralysis'. Looking back, the Spaz wasn't all that different from me. I had paralyzed muscles in my left leg, and his paralysis was in his brain.

I also now understand that many individuals with cerebral palsy have normal or above-average intelligence, but they can't express their intelligence because of their difficulties with communication.

Today, as I write these words about the Spaz, and understand that he was just a little boy trapped inside a twisted body, I feel true guilt and regret.

I will never again call him or any other person with cerebral palsy a Spaz. Seldom does life allow one the chance to go back in time and correct a wrong, but if I could go back, I would stop and talk to him each time I passed his bed.

I would listen to his attempts at communication. And I would make sure that the kid received his weekly ration of comic books.

And my final regret? I never knew his real name because I never once asked a nurse or an orderly what that name was.

Most all of today's hospitals have TVs, radios, and often wireless access to the internet so patients can watch television or supply their own entertainment with an iPad or a laptop computer. But in 1947, two years after the war ended, daily life in the boys' ward at the Orthopedic Hospital could be summed up in a single word: Boredom. And even worse than being bored, I was going to miss Christmas at home.

So how bad was it being stuck in a hospital during Christmas?

It wasn't bad; in fact, and this is something I never told my mom, the Christmas I spent in the hospital turned out to be the best Christmas I ever had.

Each day for two weeks before Christmas and the week after, some people would come into our ward pushing a big metal bin with some kind of toy or book. The silly part was that the people usually gave us toys we couldn't use, like a car that you had to roll on the floor, or a coloring book about the circus that was meant for a two-year-old, but I didn't care, it was a Christmas present. I kept all the toys I couldn't use and gave them to my brother and sister.

But I couldn't hand over the toys directly to them. In those days the hospital had a "no kids" visiting policy. I have no idea why they had that policy. And back then there were limited visiting days and hours for adults. Today, most hospitals allow you to visit any day of the week at most any hour. Why the change? Again, I haven't a clue.

Mom and dad came by once a week to visit. Each week I gave the presents to them to take home. As I said, Christmas in the hospital lasted for three weeks, but that's not the best part of this story.

One time, near the end of the toy handout, a man walked through the ward and gave each boy a real squirt gun.

As I think back, had a nurse seen what was going on, the squirt gun story would have ended before it started, but for some serendipitous reason, there was not a nurse or an orderly in sight.

I guess the staff had forgotten that there were few things on earth as dangerous as fourteen bored boys with squirt guns in their hands.

Every boy was bug-eyed, but no one cried out with excitement. It was as if all the boys had been born with the knowledge that the slightest noise would give away their hidden treasure. Everyone immediately slipped his water pistol under their pillow and waited for the magic moment to arrive.

The second the squirt gun man walked out of the ward, we pulled out our weapons from under the pillows and loaded up. In an instant we were squirting anyone or anything, we thought we could hit. With each pull of the trigger all of us giggled and shrieked with laughter.

But all the fun ended when the head nurse walked in and nearly slipped on a puddle of water.

The funniest part of the great water gun shoot-out was that other than our weekly comic book delivery, the third floor boys' ward had no privileges to revoke, so the head nurse marched up to each bed, confiscated the now empty water weapons, and stormed out of the room.

That was the greatest squirt gun fight of my life. After George the orderly finished mopping the puddles off the floor, he told me that the squirt gun man had given one to the Spaz, but the Spaz had dumped his full water pitcher all over his bed trying to load the squirt gun before the head nurse took it from him.

A closing memory of my second stay in the hospital concerns the nurses in the boys' ward who were all pretty nice except for one night nurse. I don't remember her name but she made us feel guilty if any of us pushed the nurse-call button when she was on duty. So all the boys avoided calling her except for real emergencies.

The last time I talked to her was after the best evening I had during that two month stay in the boys' ward.

The hospital was going to show a movie called Meet Me In St. Louis, and it was announced that any of the boys who were well enough to sit in a wheelchair for a couple of hours could go to the movie.

Meet Me In St. Louis was scheduled to take two hours, but it was only two weeks after my surgery and the head nurse was not positive my leg had healed well enough for me to sit in a wheelchair that long.

I begged.

I pleaded.

I cried.

Eventually she gave in. After dinner an orderly and a nurse helped me into a wheelchair—the first time I had been out of my bed since the operation—and the orderly wheeled me into an elevator, down three stories to the ground level, and into the hospital auditorium.

All around me were boys and girls lying on gurneys and propped up in wheelchairs. There were even four people along the wall inside their iron lungs. Their mirrors had been tilted so they could see the big movie screen. As I write these words, the excitement of that evening remains palpable.

The lights went down and the movie started. My eyes bugged out as I watched the Smith family talk about going to the World's Fair. People sang as they rode a trolley, and I watched Tootie and her little sister play hop scotch.

The effect on all of us was magical. For two hours I wasn't a nine-year-old boy stuck in a wheelchair with a cast on his leg, I was a member of the Smith family who lived in St. Louis during the 1904 World's Fair.

The movie was great, and there was a really cute actress who played Tootie Smith. Her name was Margaret O'Brian. And this is the best part; I didn't tell anyone, not my mom, or dad, or any of the boys in the ward, but I decided there and then that Margaret O'Brian was now my official girlfriend. Someday, when I could walk without a brace, we would go on a date, and then we would get married.

When the lights came up, the room exploded with applause and cheers and everybody was smiling and happy.

But my happiness was short lived. On the way into the elevator, the front wheel of a gurney hit my left leg and I cried out in pain. As the elevator rose to the third floor, I felt a throbbing under my cast, as if my stitches had popped open, or something even worse. I bit my lip to stop the tears. Once we reached the ward, the orderly and the night nurse lifted me onto my bed.

Before the night nurse left, I told her what had happened in the elevator and asked her for a pain pill. She shook her head and told me that if I was well enough to go to the movie, then I was well enough to sleep through the night without a pain pill.

She turned, walked away and left me there, crying softly as I tried to ignore the throbbing pain.

The next day, during morning rounds, I told Dr. Lowman that a gurney wheel had hit my cast. He lifted out the square piece of cast that the man had cut into the plaster and looked at the stitches. He told me that the incision was bleeding a little but the stitches were intact and there would be no permanent damage. Before he moved to the next bed, Doctor Lowman warned me that as I grew older, I had to be careful or I could damage all of the corrective surgery that had been done on my leg. He also told me I shouldn't play risky sports in high school, such as baseball, football, and basketball.

I was only nine years old and didn't care about playing any of those high school sports, but if another movie with Margaret O'Brian came to the hospital, I was going to see that movie and I wasn't going to let a little pain get in my way.

During and following World War II, the relatively new profession of physical therapy was faced with the dual challenge of providing rehabilitation for the large number of injured war veterans and managing the resurgence in the number of cases of poliomyelitis. As a response, in 1945, through collaboration with the American Physiotherapy Association, the National Foundation for Infantile Paralysis dedicated $1,267,600 dollars for the advancement of physical therapy for the treatment of paralytic polio.
***Physiotherapy Review,* 1945:25:79**

CHAPTER TWELVE

Recuperation, Physical Therapy, And The Joy Of Home Schooling

Following each of my surgeries at the Orthopedic Hospital, I required long periods of recuperation and physical therapy. For example, I attended weekly physical therapy sessions to teach my newly transplanted muscle, or muscles, how to do a new job.

The hospital had also given my mom some exercises for me to do at home, but two to three times each week, we still had to drive to the clinic so the professionals could work their magic on my left leg.

By the end of the 1940s, my dad had

returned to his old job at the Post Office. My mom worked part time for a caterer, and although my parents never discussed money matters around the dinner table, I felt that our family finances had improved from the early days of my illness.

As a family, we seldom ate outside our home. In the 1940s, the now ubiquitous McDonald's was a small, single hamburger stand in San Bernardino, California. Furthermore, today's family restaurants such as Applebee's, Denny's, and Round Table Pizza, didn't exist.

In fact, my only memory of eating out with the whole family was at a place called Kentucky Boy's on Pico Boulevard. My dad liked the restaurant because he had been there before with some of the men from his work. The restaurant had a long counter, shiny tables, and a waitress who took our order. But after a dinner that I thought was great, my mom informed my dad that Kentucky Boy's was a cut below her standards, and as far as I can recall, we never went back there again.

Then one glorious day, after an exhausting morning therapy session at the clinic, my mom surprised me with a lunch out at a fancy restaurant.

I do not recall the name of the restaurant, but I do remember that I ate my first Shrimp Louie salad there. That was the first of our special lunch dates, but they did not happen very often, just often enough to make me think it was a possibility after every therapy session. To this day, a giant Shrimp Louie salad ranks high on my list of memorable foods.

After that first special lunch, mom swore me to secrecy. In fact, when my brother reads this, the Shrimp Louie story might be the first time he finds out that he missed out on some outstanding culinary delights.

But enough about eating Shrimp Louie salads. In addition to my out-patient physical therapy sessions, after each of my three surgeries, once the cast was removed from my leg, a nurse would put me into a wheelchair and we would take the elevator down three stories to the ground floor where hospital's warm pool was situated.

The physical therapists had an unusual method for moving patients to, into, and out of the pool, and it remains a vivid memory.

As far as I could tell, all of the patients in the pool were disabled. Some were completely incapacitated. Other patients, like me, could get around with a brace or crutch, but without my brace my balance was so poor that walking on the wet, slippery, poolside tiles was a threat. To limit the risk of injury to disabled patients as they entered or exited the pool, the hospital installed a unique overhead track to the ceilings of the hallways that connected the pool to the hospital and the clinic.

Once patients had put on their swim suits, they were laid on what looked like highly varnished wooden table tops, and the physical therapist, or nurse, would strap the patient down to prevent falls. Now secure, the physical therapist, or nurse, would pull on a chain and the wooden stretcher would rise up to the overhead track.

The first time I was taken to the pool, I could not figure out what was going on. I did not know what the physical therapist was doing when she pulled on the chain and the wooden stretcher floated up with me on it. For a moment I was frightened that something bad would happen. But then the physical therapist pulled on a rope and the stretcher moved along like I was riding on a little train in the air that slowly moved down the long hall and turned into the pool room.

The over-head track ended over the pool and once I had arrived, the physical therapist would lower the stretcher to the water, where a man waited in the pool. The man would unbuckle me, and the pool part of my physical therapy session would begin.

I really liked the pool. The warm water helped my muscles relax, and if I held onto the the sides of the pool, the buoyancy of the water allowed me to stand up and walk around without my brace.

After my time was up at the pool, the man would put his arms under me and float me back onto the floating wooden stretcher, cinch me in, and hoist me back up to the ceiling. Then the physical therapist would pull my little train back to the boy's ward. After I dried off and before I changed into my hospital gown or my regular clothes, the physical therapist would work on my right arm and hand and left leg and foot. She would help me with exercises such as squeezing a rubber ball, and lifting small weights to strengthen the muscles of my right arm and hand,. Slowly, over the years, I recovered most of the strength that polio had taken away.

Dr. Lowman was confident I would regain seventy-five to eighty percent of the use of my right arm and hand and he was correct. But seventy-five to eighty percent strength in my right hand also means that my left hand is twenty to twenty-five percent stronger.

Today, I eat, and sign my books right handed. But if an activity requires a higher level of strength, such as twisting open a stubborn jar top, or opening a tight door, I use my left hand. To the casual observer, I use my right hand just like any normal right-handed person, but the stuck jar lids and the difficult door knobs that clutter up my world know better.

For my left leg and foot, the therapist would spend the bulk of her time teaching me to utilize the latest muscle that Doctor Lowman had just transplanted. Back in the 1940s, identifying those muscles was not an easy task. At least it was difficult for me. Today, a physical therapist could use a mild electric current to identify the muscle in question. But back then no one had thought of that method so the physical therapist would say, "Kenny, there's a new muscle attached to the front of your left foot. Now, tighten that muscle and lift your foot."

Nothing would happen, because my brain did not have a clue which muscle I was suppose to tighten.

She would rub her thumb along the scar of the latest surgery and say, "Come on, Kenny, you can do it." Then she would run her finger from the bottom of the scar to the tips of my toes along the front of my foot. "The muscle's right here. Try again. Tighten that muscle and lift your foot."

To this day I still cannot envision how anyone could tighten a single muscle by locating it with their brain. After my first two surgeries, I spent many futile months in physical therapy attempting to mentally differentiate a muscle that now lifted my left foot from one that used to wiggled my toes, or one that used to turn my left foot in or out and now lifted my foot.

Eventually, after my third surgery, something clicked in my gray matter and my brain discovered the transplanted tibialis posterior muscle just as my physical therapist had promised. The first time I tried, my left foot twitched, and then I slowly lifted my left foot, perhaps a tenth of an inch. After that breakthrough therapy session, the muscle that lifted my foot continued to get stronger and finally I could walk without a brace.

But after each operation there was more to my life than exercises and going to the clinic for physical therapy.

The best part was that when I returned home, I could play with my sister and brother. In fact, playing a game with my brother was what got me into real trouble.

What was the trouble and what was the game? To answer those questions I need to explain two unrelated items that are important to the story:

The first item? Although I was recuperating at home, my day-to-day life remained limited because I was dependent on a wheelchair to move about. I could eat at the table with the rest of the family., sit in the living room and watch TV, and take myself to the bathroom. But I was restricted to the rooms inside our house and forced to roll around looking for something to do. But bored little boys are clever. During my first week home, I discovered that my wheelchair just fit through a tight doorway that led to a narrow terrace outside of our dining room. The edge of the outdoor terrace was located about three feet away from, and two feet above, the sidewalk.

The dining room door leading to the terrace was a great discovery and for a few days I reveled in my new freedom. I sat outside in the sunshine and enjoyed the fresh air. But I was just a kid, and like all kids, after a couple days of basking and breathing, boredom returned.

The second item? While watching the Pasadena Rose Parade on TV I saw the cowboy, Monte Montana, ride his horse down the street. Sometimes his horse would stop and Monte would toss his lasso over the shoulders of a man watching on the sidelines. Each time Monte roped someone the crowd cheered.

To most, Monte Montana and a tiny outdoor terrace may not seem related, but you don't understand the mind of a bored little boy.

One day, while I was sitting on the terrace reading a comic book, my brother rode by on his bike just a few feet from where I sat. That was the moment when the disparate items came together. I could pretend to be Monte Montana, and as my brother rode his bike by me, I could toss my lasso over his shoulders.

In the blink of an eye, I had invented a new game.

Granted, I had a couple of minor details to figure out: First, how to fashion a lasso out of some old rope my dad kept in the garage, and second, how to convince my brother that riding by the terrace and getting lassoed was a great idea.

I talked over my idea with Dicky. He remembered seeing Monte Montana, too, and agreed that it sounded like a lot of fun.

Leaving me sunning on the terrace, my brother went into the garage and brought out some rope. After we measured what I thought would be more than enough, my brother asked our mom for a pair of scissors. I don't have a clue what excuse he gave her for needing the scissors, but I am pretty sure he didn't tell her that I was making a lasso so I could throw a rope around him as he rode his bike past the terrace.

Anyway, the lasso was now constructed, and I began to practice my rope tossing technique while Dicky rode back and forth trying to increase the speed of his bike.

At this point I need to insert my observation of one of the major differences between a child and an adult: A child will jump off the top of a bunk bed without any consideration for the future result. On the other hand, an adult will look down from the top bunk, realize the fall could likely cause a serious injury, and not jump. But my brother was eight and I was ten.

Having practiced our roles in the game, we agreed he should make his first pass. As my brother raced by the terrace the first time, I tossed the loop at him, but I missed. After many futile attempts, the muscles in my arms started to ache, but each time Dicky flashed by me, I became more and more determined to rope him. Eventually, after endless tries, the loop floated over his shoulders and pinned his arms to his side.

Needless to say, neither my brother nor I had considered what would happen next. Had I been older, I am sure I would have recognized the inherent danger and let go of the rope. Instead, I pulled my end. Dicky flew off his bike and crashed onto the sidewalk. His first scream told me that he was really hurt. Our mother flew out the back door and ran to my brother who was lying on the concrete. Then she spotted the rope around his shoulders. Her eyes slowly tracked the rope all the way up to my hand.

Mom looked at Dicky, and then back at me, and her expression spoke volumes. I may have been recuperating from surgery, I might even have been in some pain from the aforementioned operation, but wheelchair bound or not, I could tell that I was in deep trouble.

Mom helped my little brother stand up and asked him where it hurt. When she barely touched his shoulder with her finger he screamed.

Without taking her eyes off my brother, mom shook her head and said, "Kenny, don't you move off that terrace. I'm taking your brother to the doctor, but before I go, I'm calling your father to tell him to come home at once. While you wait for him, I want you to think about what you just did to your little brother."

Mom walked my brother, who was obviously in pain, to the garage, opened the door, and carefully placed him on the front seat of our car.

Then she ran back into our house. After a minute she ran out the back door with her purse. When she reached our car she stopped, looked at me, and yelled, "Your father told me he'll be home in ten minutes. Don't you dare move until he gets here. Tonight at dinner, we'll both be looking for an explanation concerning your behavior today. Do I make myself clear?"

"Yes, mom."

That evening, during dinner, my dad served as both judge and jury. Mom was the prosecutor and before I could blink my eyes, I was convicted of a crime called, "A boy your age should have known better." My sentence? All my TV privileges were taken away for two weeks.

My brother's sentence was a broken collar bone. His shoulder and arm were immobilized in a plaster cast for a month while I remained stuck in my wheel chair.

The real loser of my new game? My brother, and our long-suffering mom who was now stuck with two restless boys who could not leave the house.

To this day, whenever the lassoing story of my brother is brought up at a family gathering, I look sheepishly at him and he grimaces at the memory of the pain when his shoulder hit the concrete sidewalk.

As I've said more than once, there's nothing more dangerous than little boys with time on their hands and nothing to do.

Throughout life, unexpected events happen, or seemly unimportant decisions are made that completely reshape the future. And those shifts in the future vary from the not-so-good to the truly miraculous.

In my case, the not-so-good? I caught polio when I was only five and my potential as an enthusiastic student through my high school graduation and beyond was never fully realized.

My elementary school years were interrupted by two to four trips per week to the physical therapist. During those years I missed approximately four to eight hours of formal education each week, and I never recovered my lost classroom time. The Los Angeles school system did all it could to fill in the gaps in my education and because of that diligence my polio story wouldn't be complete without a mention of my one and only experience of being taught at home by an official Los Angeles School District home-school teacher. I gained the honor of a visit from a home teacher because my hospital stay took place from mid-December through January, causing me to miss a month and a half of school.

It's strange, but I cannot recall my home school teacher's name. I do remember that the teacher was a woman and that she came to my house every Monday, Wednesday, and Friday afternoon for two hours.

What did I learn? Not very much I am afraid. Beyond the history of Burma up to the Japanese invasion in 1938, there's not much else that I recall, except that the country of Burma evolved from the people who inhabited the Irrawaddy Valley in the 2nd century BCE. Perhaps the memory of Burma's early history stuck in my head because of that valley's name, Irrawaddy.

As I reached adulthood, the fact that the country of Burma had changed its' name to Myanmar took me a long time to accept.

My home teacher may have tried to teach me math, or English, and American History, but to the best of my recollection, the country of Burma is all I can recall, not those picky little things like correct punctuation. And that could be the reason why the group of writers I meet with every two weeks have dubbed me, "The King of the Misplaced Apostrophe."

Truthfully, I'm not proud of my "King of the Misplaced Apostrophe" title. In my case, to put it simply, the more school I missed, the less I missed school. It was as if my one and only goal in life, from the first day I met Doctor Lowman, was to be able to walk with a normal gait by the time I reached sixteen. And as I look back, I think that was about all that my teachers and parents expected of me.

In grammar school, I was always the crippled kid in class. As such, I felt that my teachers did not expect as much from me as they did from their healthy students. So, as my teachers demanded less and less from me, I went along and accepted their expectations as my lot in life.

My parents made great sacrifices, for which I owe them more than my ability to walk normally. I'm in debt to them for my adult life. But, and this is a big but, I am positive that neither my father nor my mother expected as much from me as they did from my sister or brother. For example, my sister and brother were both consistently encouraged to go on to college, but I cannot recall my mom or dad ever urging me to further my education beyond a high school diploma.

Not long after I earned that high school diploma, I got a job with the Pacific Bell Telephone company to work inside, in one of its central offices, maintaining an electro-mechanical forerunner to today's computer systems. At the time, I was pleased with my career decision because the Pacific Bell offered me a well-paying position, job stability, and benefits, and, even more important to me, the opportunity for advancement.

However, during one of my early work evaluations, my supervisor informed me that because I had a "bad" leg, I could never work outside, climb poles, and therefore would not be considered for promotion to management at Pac Bell. He stated that the company required all managerial candidates have experience with both the inside and outside company disciplines.

His dictum didn't surprise me. I had faced limitations caused by polio most of my life, so I decided that working as a technician in the central office would present me with enough of a challenge. I accepted his statement that I would never be promoted and settled down to do my job working with the switching system that provided dial tone, and then switched calls to the desired numbers.

Suddenly, the formal education that I had spent much of my childhood avoiding, became important to me. During my first decade at Pacific Bell, I spent nearly two years in eight-hour-a-day classes to achieve the level of technical expertise required to work with the various switching systems, Through those years of training, I slowly worked my way up the technical ladder of an increasingly complex company.

I reached the top step of the technical

ladder when my boss assigned me as the sole person with the responsibility to install, and activate the first digital carrier system in Southern California.

During digital carrier training, I was stunned by the elegant beauty and life changing concepts of digital electronics. I recognized how the simple idea of something being turned on or off would ultimately change the world we live in.

In today's society, just about every item we use, from computers, to iPads, cars, sound systems, smart phones, TV's, CD's, DVD's, movies, and nearly everything else you can think of works by using the digital concept.

My upward mobility changed some years after my successful digital carrier installation, when I was in my early thirties. Pacific Bell needed more managers, and my supervisor sent me to a special evaluation session in Sacramento called the Personal Assessment Review, or PAR.

Over the three-day period I joined with nineteen others in a series of workshops, tests, and cleverly constructed projects designed to uncover the latent intellectual promise that could be hidden in each PAR participant.

In one of the projects, the twenty participants were given four hours to solve the identical hypothetical problem. But if, during those four hours, a participant felt the need to ask a question, he or she had to write the question down and hand the paper to the proctor. The proctor would look at the question and write down the answer. That way, each participant's solution to the identical problem would be theirs and theirs alone, unassisted by the input of questions and answers from the other participants.

Weeks later, when I received my results from PAR, I was stunned. My numbers were off the chart, and I was told by an impartial observer, for the first time in my life, that I was smarter than the average bear.

Throughout our early years of marriage, Arlene had tried everything she could think of to convince me that I had hidden talents, but no matter how hard she worked, it took that Pac Bell PAR session, when I was over thirty, to make me realize that I had the intelligence to accomplish anything I wanted to do.

After twenty-five years of living with limited expectations, those three days in Sacramento returned the confidence that had vanished when the polio virus had paralyzed my leg and arm.

Six months later I was promoted. Eight years passed and I was promoted again taking over the management responsibility for all inside telephone service from the Golden Gate Bridge to near the Oregon border. The area encompassed five counties. I managed one hundred and thirty employees who drove seventy motor vehicles to maintain sixty-three central offices that ran twenty-four hours a day, seven days a week, three hundred and sixty-five days a year.

Looking back, I harbor no anger toward my parents because they did what they thought was right based on what was known in the 1940s, and 1950s. More simply stated, when they found themselves up to their armpits in alligators, it was hard for them to remember that they were there to drain the swamp.

It was Pacific Bell who gave me the confidence to move forward, but there was other happenings that changed my life. For that we need to go back before I graduated from high school, to a wonderful, serendipitous event that reshaped the rest of my life.

As a teen, I was very shy, and as previously stated, lacked confidence.

That all changed one day when a neighborhood buddy, Bill, asked me to attend party at his girlfriend Joyce's house because the gathering was short one male.

During the party I met Arlene. She had blonde hair, the sweetest smile, and the bluest eyes I had ever seen. It is interesting to note that Arlene had never known me when I wore a brace, or a lift on my heel. As we danced and talked, I came to realize that I really liked her. When the party was over, I took one last look at her mesmerizing blue eyes and said goodbye.

For the next couple of months every time I

thought of Arlene, I battled with my lack of self-confidence but never summoned up enough courage to call her for a date.

Bill and Joyce saved the day, jump-started my lack of courage when they called me and asked if Arlene and I wanted to go with them on a double date to a movie.

That was our first date. I don't remember the name of the movie, because all I saw was Arlene.

After we dated for a couple of years we became engaged and a year later, married. It is obvious that our marriage was the right decision for us. We recently celebrated our 57th wedding anniversary, providing concrete proof that love-at-first-sight really does happen.

Over our years of marriage, Arlene and I raised three marvelous children and once they were married, we were thrilled to become the grandparents of four. We are now the great-grandparents of eight, soon to be nine.

Once I became a parent, I was driven to be sure that our children would not suffer from limited expectations. To achieve that goal, we encouraged our three children to do their very best at grammar school, middle school, high school, and to attend college. To inspire them to reach those goals, we promised each one that after high school and two years at our local junior college, we would pay all expenses for them to attend the university or college of their choice, anywhere in the world.

The results? Two undergraduate degrees, one master's degree, and a highly successful graphic artist who attended the Art Center College of Design in Pasadena, California.

And we continue to motivate our four grandchildren. Those results? Three undergraduate degrees and a master's degree.

Finally, we have set up a college fund program for our eight great-grandchildren and contribute an annual sum to each child on their birthday.

So if you still have a question if you should motivate your children or your nieces, or nephews to achieve the most they can in life, and to excel at all levels of education to achieve an undergraduate degree, my answer is encompassed in three simple words—do it now!

"The hospital was like a summer camp for polios. Surgeries were planned. You booked a spot in advance." Rather than looking forward to carefree summers, these young men and women dreaded the approach of the surgery season.
***Living With Polio,* Daniel J. Wilson**

CHAPTER THIRTEEN

1949—Age 11—Third Surgery
I'm eleven now and I'm going into the hospital for my third operation.
This time Doctor Lowman tells me he is going to drill a hole through a bone in my left leg and then move a muscle from the back of my leg, through the hole, and connect it to the front of my left foot. He thinks this will finally do the trick
I hope it works this time so I can stop wearing my brace.
My dad has to work so mom drives me to the hospital and stays with me until a nurse tells my mom it is time to go.
We take the same elevator up to the third floor.
We walk past the iron lung ward and it looks like there are still lots of iron lungs with people stuck inside.
As we walk toward the boys' ward, the

nurse says, "Is this your first time at the Orthopedic Hospital?"

I shake my head. "No. This is my third operation.

She says, "I see you wear a brace. Will this operation correct that?"

"I hope so."

"Who is your doctor?"

"Doctor Lowman."

"My goodness. He's the top man."

Before I say anything we pass the crib with the Spaz and walk into the ward.

The nurse says, "Kenny, your bed's the empty one by the window."

Mom will be happy.

The nurse says, "I'll need your brace." She starts to close the curtains around my bed. "And—"

I tell her, "I know. Just get it over with."

Last operation, George, the nice orderly, told me that all the boys have to get an enema before surgery 'cause if they don't, while they're asleep, they could poop all over the doctors.

Later, I look at the other boys in the ward. Most of them are younger than me. Then I see Juan, just a couple of beds away.

I wave and he waves back.

Juan is about my age.

I check out the night stand next to my bed to see if anything has changed since the last time.

Everything looks the same. Sitting on the top is a metal pitcher full of water and a couple of paper cups. Paper cups are new. Inside the drawer is a spit bowl that I'll use when I brush my teeth. I set my tooth brush and tooth paste inside the spit bowl. Underneath the drawer are two shelves. On the first shelf sits my urinal. Below that is my bedpan.

We have a TV set at home, but the boys' ward still doesn't have a TV or a radio, so we still don't have anything to do but lay on our beds and read or talk.

I am eleven now so mostly I read real books, not comics. My favorite book is about a man who is a master deep sea diver looking for sunken treasures. The story tells about the dangers of the 'bends', something bad that happens to your blood if you come up from the bottom of the sea too fast.

Early next morning an orderly pushes me on a gurney down the hall to my third operation.

Everything inside the operating room looks the same, except this time, the black mask doesn't smell as bad.

I go to sleep and then wake up.

Mom and dad are there. Mom holds me down and says, "Don't sit up too fast or you'll be sick."

She helps me up and my dad pulls back the sheet so I can see my cast. It is bigger and

longer than the last time and goes from above my knee to my toes.
After a couple of seconds I fall asleep. When I wake up I am back in my boys' ward bed.
The next day the guy with the saw comes by my bed and tells me he is going to cut out a hole on the left side of the cast.
He says, "Don't worry, it won't hurt."
I tell him, "I know. I've done this before. How big is the hole?"
He checks a piece of paper. "Four inches along the foot in front of the ankle bone and then up the leg for another five inches."
"Wow, that's nine inches. That's a lot longer than my other operations."
"Kid, I don't know about that, but this incision is a long one alright."
When he finishes, he takes out two pieces of the cast and I can see inside. There are lots of bloody black stitches that go along my foot and up my ankle.
The man sticks the pieces back and runs some tape across the cast to hold the pieces in.
The next day, Doctor Lowman and a bunch of doctors come by for morning rounds.
Doctor Lowman says, "Good morning, Kenny. Let's have a look at your leg."
He and the other doctors talk about my operation for a long time, and how Doctor Lowman drilled a hole in something called my tibia.

Doctor Lowman says, "The incision looks good, Kenny. No infection. See you tomorrow morning."

The bunch of doctors move to the next bed.

Except for morning rounds and the nurse checking your chart to make sure you have had a BM, not much else happens in the boys' ward unless it is Monday when the comic book man comes by, or when one of the boys is taken by a gurney down the hall for his operation.

It's been two weeks since my operation. My leg feels better.

Right after visiting hours are over is when Charlie starts the next squirt gun story.

First, you got to know that Charlie's bed is between my bed and Juan's.

Then, during visiting hours, I see Charlie's dad give him a squirt gun.

Charlie thanks his dad, winks at me, and sticks the squirt gun under his pillow.

I don't think any of the other boys who see that Charlie has a squirt gun were here during the giant boys' ward squirt gun fight two years ago.

My friend Juan, besides having a bad blood thing, is deaf. Stuck to the front of his hospital gown is a hearing aid. His hearing aid is a small box about the size of a deck of cards with a little round circle in the center. There are two wires that go from the box to little ear pieces that Juan sticks into his ears. If those ear pieces are not in his ears, or the hearing aid isn't working, Juan can't hear a thing.

After visiting hours are over I watch Charlie pull his squirt gun from under his pillow and he fills it from his water pitcher.

Then Charlie waits for two things to happen: for the ward nurse to leave the ward and for Juan to take off his hearing aid so he can wash his face before dinner.

The nurse says, "Boys, dinner will be served in a few minutes. It's time to wash your hands and face."

The nurse leaves the ward.

Juan turns his hearing aid off and pulls out his ear pieces so he can wash his face and hands.

Charlie knows that once Juan's hearing aid is off, he can't hear a word so he yells to the rest of the boys in the ward that he is going to take out Juan's hearing aid with a single shot from his squirt gun.

Every boy in the ward stops what he is doing, sets down his comic book and stares at Juan.

Juan finishes washing his face, and after he sticks in his ear pieces and turns on his hearing aid, Charlie calls Juan's name.

Juan turns toward Charlie.

Charlie's aim is perfect. A solid stream of water hits the dead center of Juan's hearing aid.

Juan screams, pulls out his little speakers, and yells a bunch of Spanish words at Charlie.
Then Juan reaches into the drawer of his night stand and takes out a tiny screwdriver. He opens the back of the hearing aid case, taps it a couple of times to dump any water out, and then he sets the case on the warm window sill above his head. An hour goes by and Juan takes his dry hearing aid case, replaces the cover, tightens the tiny screws, sticks the ear pieces back in his ears and opens his comic book.
That's when Charlie takes out his squirt gun again and calls Juan's name.
Without thinking, Juan turns toward Charlie's voice, and again his hearing aid case ends up in the stream of water from Charlie's squirt gun. Juan tries to cover the hearing aid case with his hand but he is too late 'cause the water has already hit it.
Now Juan is really mad. He pushes his nurse-call button.
Charlie panics and hides his squirt gun under his mattress.
The nurse comes in, talks with Juan, shakes her head, turns and tells Charlie to hand over his squirt gun.
All the boys in the ward can see the jig is up, and we all start to read our comic books.

Charlie reaches under his mattress and hands over his weapon.
The nurse shouts, "Let this be a warning to all of you. If anyone in this ward ever shoots water at Juan's hearing aid again, I will make sure the comic book man skips this ward for the next two months."
An hour later, after the sun has dried out Juan's hearing aid case a second time, he screws it back together, pulls out an old comic book, and pretends nothing ever happened.
The nurse really scares all the boys 'cause nobody ever even looks at Juan's hearing aid again.

During my third surgery stay at the Orthopedic Hospital I learned that Juan had hemophilia. One night, after the lights went out, Juan told me that he had been in and out of the Orthopedic Hospital most of his life.

He was forced to spend most of his days in bed to protect him from falling down. If he cut himself, or even worse, started to bleed internally, the doctors wouldn't be able to stop the bleeding and he could die. Prior to the 1960s, when more effective treatment became available, the life expectancy for a hemophiliac like Juan was a brief eleven years.

As I looked back at 1949, I realized that Juan, who was about my age, had most likely reached, or exceeded his predicted life expectancy during the weeks that followed my third surgery.

Except for the Spaz, Juan was my only constant in the boys' ward during two of my first three operations, and although I couldn't, or wouldn't have stopped Charlie from disabling Juan's hearing aid with his squirt gun, today I can't help but feel a little guilty for standing by and letting him torment my friend that way.

Except for Charlie's squirt gun bit, over the one hundred and twelve days that Juan and I were together in the boys' ward, I never once heard him complain about anything. I'm positive that had Juan and I had attended the same elementary school, and neither of us could play any sports, he and I would have just walked around the playground during recess and talked, just like we did in the hospital most every night after the lights went out.

Patients had to find ways to occupy their abundant free time. Children and adolescents needed to expend some of their excess energy, especially once they became mobile. There was always something to complain about. There were holidays to celebrate, at home if one was lucky, in the hospital if one was not. There was school to attend, or lessons to keep up with. There were visits from family and friends to anticipate, and their departure to dread. And, finally, one could look forward to being discharged and returning home after weeks, perhaps months of hospitalization.
Living With Polio, **Daniel J. Wilson**

CHAPTER FOURTEEN

The Third Floor Boys' Ward

Before writing this memoir, I never gave a second thought to the ward where I had spent so much of life during my formative years. Over the past sixty years, whenever I visited a friend or relative in a hospital, I noticed that they were staying in a semi-private (a nice way to say a two-person) room. I began to wonder why I, as a child, had been relegated to a fourteen-bed ward in the Orthopedic Hospital.

Had my family been so poor that they couldn't afford a semi-private room for me?

In the process of writing this book I did some research into hospitals and discovered the following answers to that question:

First, during the 1940s and 1950s, the years I was in and out of the Orthopedic Hospital, multi-bed wards were the standard arrangement for all hospitals.

In fact, at that time, hospital design was just beginning to evolve from the original ward concept to the semi-private and private room arrangement with which we are familiar with today.

But if semi-private rooms are today's standard, just how long did the ward concept reign?

To truly understand the ward to private room evolution, you will require a bit of history on hospital construction. For that, we need return all the way back to the ninth century when Charlemagne ruled.

During that era, most hospitals were built as a single room ward and attached to a cathedral. Monks provided health care to the poor while the rich were attended in their homes, or castles, by physicians.

Hospitals changed very little between the time of Charlemagne and the mid-20th century. The first hospital in North America, the Hotel-Dieu (House of God) was built in Quebec in 1639 as a single ten bed ward near a cathedral.

As hospitals and medical practices improved, hospital facilities became the first choice for the wealthy as well as the poor, so the demand for private rooms in public hospitals increased. However, multi-bed wards continued to be the main component of new hospital construction even though the number of patients per ward was declining. By 1950, when the St. Thomas Hospital in London was remodeled, the largest ward contained only four beds.

To put it simply, in the 1940s and 1950s, I spent all of my hospital days in a fourteen-bed ward because multi-bed wards were the hospital standard.

From my viewpoint, the major negative of staying in a multi-bed ward was the total lack of privacy. But on the positive side, there was the opportunity for non-stop social interaction between patients.

A classic example of some real social interactions were the two squirt gun affairs I have previously recounted in the boys' ward. Even though I now look upon the attack on Juan's hearing aid with remorse, I'd be lying if I said that those events did not raise our spirits. Why? Because shooting water from bed to bed was the only way we could solve the main problem with the boys' ward—all of us were trapped in our beds.

We couldn't get up to go to the bathroom.

We couldn't go from bed to bed to trade comics.

We couldn't walk over to the window to peek at the world that existed outside our cloistered walls.

And because our beds were set about ten feet apart, we had no direct physical contact with each other.

For example, one time I got so mad at the boy in the next bed that I tore out a comic book page, soaked it in water, and threw a wet paper wad at him.

I didn't want to hurt him, just hit him with it to let him know I was mad. But I missed him and the evidence of my failed attempt ended up on the floor. Five minutes later a nurse noticed the wad and picked it up.

Trust me, I learned quickly that a nurse didn't have to be a female Sherlock Holmes to deduce that the paper wad had come from my bed. She reported my attack to the head nurse, who made sure that my bed was passed by during the next comic book delivery.

As I have stated in previous chapters, we had so little to do in the boys' ward that, beyond canceling a week of comics or chewing you out, there wasn't much a nurse could do to punish us.

Because three out of four of my hospitalizations occurred during summers, there was no schooling offered during my stays, and I do not recall attempts at any type of schooling during my hospitalization over the 1947 Christmas season.

But I'm not criticizing the hospital for not setting up a school in the boys' ward. The thought of trying to formally educate fourteen boys, aged five to thirteen, who were moving in and out of the ward at the rate of one to two per week, seems to me to be an insurmountable task.

At this point you might ask: Just what did we do to fill our days on the third floor?

The answer—the daily routine in the ward was the only thing we could count on to keep us busy.

First, the lights would come on and a nurse would say, "Good morning, boys. Breakfast will be served in a few minutes."

As soon as she left, most of us would pee into our urinal and scoot it down toward the ends of our beds, open ends pointed away.

Then we would eat breakfast.

What were we served?

I have tried to recall a breakfast, or any meal, and couldn't come up with a single mental picture. Either that means that my memory is failing, or the hospital food served each day was the least memorable food in history. Knowing how much I love food and wine today, I would put my money on the least memorable food theory.

After breakfast, we would brush our teeth and leave our filled spit pans on our night stands.

Next, it was time for morning rounds. I can't say what the rest of the boys did, but I watched Doctor Lowman and the other doctors move from bed to bed. At each stop they would read the chart that hung at the end of each bed, check out the boy's cast, talk to the boy, and then move to the next bed. On a good day, the excitement of morning rounds could last as much as an hour.

After morning rounds, the head nurse would make her rounds of the ward. She would review the chart at the end of each bed, checking for bowel movements. She would talk with each boy who was late with his BM and make sure he understood that if something didn't happen soon, the dreaded enema would be the next step.

After the head nurses rounds we had a few minutes to read or talk before lunch.

After lunch, we would read or talk until a nurse came to the bed and pulled the curtain for a sponge bath. Feeling clean was great, but I always got embarrassed when she washed around my private parts.

Usually, after the nurse finished with the sponge bath, George, the orderly, would come through the ward with a big mop to clean the floor. He would always stop by each boy and talk for a minute.

Once a week, George would bring in his floor polisher and shine up the floors. That was always fun to watch and would take up at least an hour to finish waxing the ward floor.

The rest of the afternoon was used for physical therapy. Juan, the only boy who was allowed out of bed, would exercise in the ward. After a nurse helped him out of bed, a therapist would hold onto him and walk him slowly up and down between the rows of beds until Juan got tired. Those of us who had undergone surgeries and had their casts removed would be rolled in wheel chairs for physical therapy on the first floor. I followed that routine after my first and second operations, but after the third one, Doctor Lowman told me that because of the length of my incision, I wouldn't start physical therapy until after I returned home.

After physical therapy, we'd eat dinner.

Once dinner was done we'd read comics, or books, or talk.

About nine the lights would go out and we'd go to sleep.

Every couple of days, one of the boys would be helped into a wheel chair and go home. Then an orderly would change the sheets and a new boy would be moved into the empty bed.

During my two hundred and twenty-five days of hospitalization, I don't recall ever seeing an empty bed in the ward when the lights went out for the night. And except for Juan and the Spaz, all the boys in the ward were there for operations to repair damage caused by the polio virus.

I almost forgot the excitement we had every Monday when the comic book man arrived. In real time, his visit to the ward lasted no more than fifteen minutes, but the comic books he left us were like pieces of treasure and gave all of us something to occupy ourselves for days.

So there you have it. Another busy day in the third floor boys' ward at the Orthopedic Hospital through the 1940s, and 1950s.

The National Foundation for Infantile Paralysis revolutionized fundraising and the perception of disease in America using "poster children" and the March of Dimes to raise hundreds of millions of dollars from a vast army of contributors (instead of a few well-heeled benefactors), creating what is considered by the author to be the largest research and rehabilitation network in the history of medicine.
http://www.comminit.com/polio/node/185038

CHAPTER FIFTEEN

From The Georgia Warm Springs To The March Of Dimes

You may recall that chapter five ended with my mom walking down the hall of the clinic to the office of the National Foundation for Infantile Paralysis (NFIP), where she applied for financial assistance.

The nationwide NFIP guidelines suggested that financial aid was to be given to "any family which would have to lower its standard of living by paying the total costs of medical and hospital care."

My mom, who at the time of her application was living on an army private's pay and had a total of fifty cents in her purse, was not surprised that the local NFIP chapter would approve her request for aid.

Thus began my family's ten year relationship with the NFIP, an organization that, by the early 1950s, was providing financial assistance to more than 72,000 polio victims at an annual cost to the foundation of more than twenty-six million dollars. In the 1950s that was a lot of money. The NFIP assisted thousands of polio victims, but to the best of my recollection, no one in my family, including myself, ever thought to ask:

Who is the NFIP?

And where did an organization that rich come from?

And where did they get all that money?

The answers to those questions begins in the fall of 1924, when Franklin Delano Roosevelt's old Harvard chum, George Peabody, told him about a Georgia man, Lewis Joseph, who had contracted polio about the same time as FDR. Peabody told Roosevelt that Joseph was now able to walk.

Peabody extolled the virtues of the Georgia hot springs where Joseph had restored the muscles of his legs to the point that he could now walk aided only by a cane, but Peabody did not tell FDR the complete story. What Peabody neglected to mention was that he was a part owner of the hot springs and that the resort was nearly bankrupt.

Roosevelt was a practical man and a highly successful politician, but when it came to his useless legs, which had been paralyzed by polio in 1921, he was vulnerable and credulous. With hope springing that he would someday walk again, he traveled hundreds of miles south to the dilapidated resort in Georgia. Once Roosevelt arrived, Joseph took FDR to the pool and showed him he could move around, almost walk without braces, in the four-foot-deep pool of warm water.

During that initial visit, it was as if everything Roosevelt viewed was through rose-colored glasses. He was positive he had found the place where he could finally cure his withered legs.

FDR ignored the unpaved roads, the dilapidated buildings that made up the Meriwether Inn, the separate facilities for "white" and "colored" in the adjacent town. He declared the area, "Really beautiful country."

His wife, Eleanor, described her first impression of the Warm Springs area differently in her memoir, *This I Remember*. "The Meriwether Inn was a dump. Our personal cottage was so flimsy that one could look through the cracks and see daylight. Rural southern life seemed hard and poor and ugly. The racism was appalling and the natives, though friendly, were far too primitive for my tastes."

Eleanor immediately returned to New York while Franklin spent several weeks at the resort.

In 1926, Roosevelt took a leap of faith and spent two-thirds of his personal fortune to purchase, and restore the resort because there he felt comfortable taking off his braces, exposing his withered legs to the sun, and "walking" in the warm, buoyant waters of the mineral pool.

As the fame of Warm Springs spread, polio patients seeking a cure flocked to the resort. Much later, Roosevelt built a cottage there that would become the "Georgia White House" during his long presidency. It was there that he died in 1945.

Once FDR signed the real estate contract, Roosevelt's law partner, Basil O'Conner, converted the property into a nonprofit organization called the Georgia Warm Springs Foundation.

In 1928, when Roosevelt ran for Governor of New York, Basil O'Conner reluctantly took over the reins of the Georgia Warm Springs Foundation, but did so with indifference toward the charitable foundation. Other than his business relationship with FDR, he had never exhibited the slightest interest in helping the victims of polio, later stating in Good Housekeeping magazine, "My decision (to assume control of the Georgia Warm Springs Foundation) had no more emotional significance than taking over several file folders of unfinished business for a colleague who had embarked on a new project that would keep him overly busy."

But as time passed, O'Conner's view of the organization changed, and he made the treatment of polio patients his top priority over the next thirty years of his life. At times, his dedication to the cause was not enough. During the depression, annual contributions to the Georgia Warm Springs Foundation fell from $369,000 in 1929 to a paltry $30,000 by 1932. With no funds, new patients had to be turned away. To save the nearly bankrupt Georgia Warm Springs Foundation, O'Conner contacted a public relations genius named Carl Byoir and begged him to save President Roosevelt's foundation.

To boost fundraising, Byoir came up with a simple but brilliant idea—an annual nationwide party to celebrate newly-elected President Roosevelt's birthday each January 29th. Byoir personally called every newspaper publisher in the U.S. and asked him to nominate a local FDR Birthday Ball chairman (a tactic United Way uses today) and in turn, this made news.

Later, Byoir mused, "When you set out to influence and persuade people to action, when the campaign is tremendous, nationwide in scope, don't think that it just happens; something has to be done to get millions of people to think the thought you want them to think and then to get them to act on that thought."

Byoir's slogan for the party, "We Dance So That Others Might Walk" galvanized the American public. On the night of January 29th, more than 6,000 parties were held across America and the first year the foundation raised over one million dollars from the one-day event.

By 1938, the tie between Roosevelt's name and the Georgia Warm Springs Foundation had become so politically partisan that Roosevelt decided to rename his organization the National Foundation for Infantile Paralysis (NFIP), and placed his old friend and law partner, Basil O'Conner, as the director.

The new foundation faced enormous start-up expenses and O'Conner immediately realized that a one-day party would never cover all the financial needs required for his three-pronged approach for the organization which were: to assist existing polio patients, to conduct much needed research to find a vaccine, and to convince the American public that polio was the number one health threat in the United States.

During an early brain-storming session, Eddie Cantor, the famous movie and radio comedian, came up with a serendipitous idea called the March of Dimes. At that time, movie theaters showed a weekly short between features to give movie patrons a look at the previous week's news events. It was called the March of Time.

Cantor was a great judge of how to reach audiences, and he liked the verbal tie between the March of Times and the March of Dimes. He further suggested to O'Conner that they should tell contributors to mail their dimes directly to President Roosevelt at the White House. O'Conner pitched Cantor's off-the-wall idea to Roosevelt, and to his amazement, the president agreed.

No one knew what to expect. On the first day of the fundraiser, the White House mail room received 30,000 letters, followed by 50,000 the next day, and 150,000 on the third. Sacks of mail filled the halls of the White House mailroom. On top of the avalanche of letters, the counting of the enclosed dimes became impossible. Eventually the coins were shoveled onto a scale to be weighed before being sent to the Treasury Department.

It took weeks to clear up the mail room mess, but over 2,680,000 dimes were received along with thousands of checks and bills.From that initial campaign, the fund-raising section of NFIP would be known as the March of Dimes.

Now, with sufficient funding, O'Conner was able to organize the NFIP in the way he required to accomplish his longterm goals.

His first task was to create a network of local chapters that could raise money and deliver aid. During his tenure, he established more than 3,100 county chapters throughout the United States.

The foundation also set up a wing to fund research into a vaccine to protect future generations from the crippling disease.

Finally, the NFIP set up a public relations team that produced heart-rending posters of young polio victims with their braces, or children trapped inside iron lungs.

The March of Dimes turned out to be one of the most successful fundraising operations in American history. It succeeded by asking for and receiving small contributions from everyone—old and young—rich or poor.

After Roosevelt's death in April of 1945, the U. S. mint struck a new dime with Roosevelt's profile on one side. The Roosevelt dime was released in January of 1946, specifically for the annual March of Dimes campaign.

Even though the March of Dimes was one of the most successful fund-raising campaigns in American history, the 415,624 documented cases of polio that occurred between 1937 to 1955 created a tidal wave of paralyzed patients that taxed the NFIP and the vast American medical system, to their breaking points.

Health insurance as we know it today did not exist, so each time a patient visited a doctor, or attended physical therapy, or underwent surgery, there was out-of-pocket cost. In my case, I went to physical therapy sessions three times each week, month after month, year after year, for years. But as my mother learned during our initial visit to the clinic in 1943, all of my medical expenses, except for braces, would be covered by the NFIP.

From 1938 through the approval of the Salk vaccine in 1955, the NFIP spent $233 million on polio patient care, providing significant foundation aid to more than 80 percent of America's polio patients. That's an amazing accomplishment for a non-profit organization founded only seventeen years earlier. I'm not overstating the facts to say that without the continued assistance of the NFIP, my family of five would have left the table with half-empty stomachs.

But as we all know, real life is not a fairy tale, and sometimes a charitable foundation's story does not end with, "and they lived happily ever after."

The NFIP and Basil O'Conner ran into an unexpected problem once the Salk and Sabin vaccines were introduced. The dreaded polio epidemics that had once ravaged the United States virtually disappeared. By 1958, the NFIP faced the reality that its organization had reached the point where their raison d'être was no longer valid and Basil O'Connor announced the Foundation's new mission: the prevention of birth defects.

In 1976, the NFIP changed its name to the March of Dimes for Birth Defects Foundation,

and in 2007 the name changed again to the March of Dimes Foundation.
Over the years, I watched "my" NFIP, or the March of Dimes, change its name and goals through what seemed to be a life and death struggle to remain a viable organization. But millions, including me, continue to contribute to their annual campaigns. In my case, a contribution is an easy decision because no matter how long I live, or how much I give, I will never give enough to pay them back for my life.

Leg lengthening or shortening involves a variety of surgical procedures used to correct legs of unequal lengths, a condition referred to as limb length discrepancy (LLD). LLD occurs because a leg bone grows more slowly in one leg than the other leg. Surgical treatment is indicated for discrepancies exceeding one inch (2.5 CM). Leg lengthening or shortening surgery is usually recommended for severe unequal leg lengths resulting from poliomyelitis, cerebral palsy, or septic arthritis.
www.surgeryencyclipedia.com–2014

CHAPTER SIXTEEN

1951—Age 13—Fourth Surgery
A loud noise wakes me up.
I pull the covers off my head and peek out the window.
The sky is dark.
I shudder 'cause I know what's going to happen to me in a couple of minutes.
I look around.
All the other boys in the ward are asleep, except for the whiner in the bed next to me.
He isn't a bad kid, but he's only six or seven and so scared he wet his bed.
After the orderly takes me he'll come back and pick up the whiner for his first operation.

I'm thirteen and the oldest kid in the ward, but I don't talk to the whiner 'cause we're both scared.
Why am I scared? 'cause after three operations I know what's going to happen.
Yesterday my mom and dad checked me in and waved goodbye.
I acted brave and waved back, but when the nurse walked me into the elevator all the bad memories came back.
I'm thirteen and don't cry anymore, but as the elevator went up to the third floor, a couple of tears fell down my freckled face.
Why did I cry?
I knew that after the operation my leg will hurt for a long time and I'll have to use a bedpan again.
I wondered if will Juan be there?
I hoped so 'cause I wanted to know someone besides the Spaz.
When we reached the boy's ward, we passed the Spaz. He was bigger but he still spit all over his bed and the floor.
The nurse showed me to a bed by the window. I jumped on it and looked around.
No Juan.
Nobody I knew.
After dinner the lights went out and I slept until that car honked its horn.
I hear a squeaky wheel on a gurney rolling down the dark hall. Someone is coming for me. George and a nurse push the gurney

next to my bed. George smiles and says, "Good morning, Kenny. Nice to see you again."

The nurse says, "Are you ready?"

I say, "Yes."

They lift me onto the gurney and push me down the hall. We pass the room that still has people living inside their iron lungs. At the end of the hall George holds the door open and the nurse rolls me into the operating room. Some people lift me onto a table. Above me is the same bright operating room light.

I look around and see Doctor Lowman. He walks over and says, "Kenny, this will be your last surgery. It's been a long road since our first meeting in the clinic. Do you recall? We shook hands after I told you that you would walk with a normal gait, and this operation will finally get you there. Now close your eyes, be brave and we'll get to work."

I cheat and keep one eye open long enough to see the black rubber mask cover my face. A voice behind me says, "Kenny, start counting backwards from one hundred."

I say, "One hundred."

I wonder if I'll finally get to wear tennis shoes.

"Ninety-nine."

I wonder how long it will take to make my legs the same.

"Ninety-eight."
I wonder if the hospital will let Dicky and Pat in to see me.
Ninety-seven."
I wonder if the kids at school will ever stop calling me . . .

Looking back, it seemed that my trepidation grew with each progressive surgery and the ensuing hospitalizations. So how did I, a thirteen year old boy, cope with fear after my last surgery?

Each night, once the lights went off, I would lie on my stomach and cover my head with a blanket so tight that only my nose stuck out. Did I really feel that hiding my head under a blanket would somehow protect me? To this day, I don't know the answer, but I do know tthe blanket over my head made me feel secure.

Secure from what?

I don't have the answer to that question either, but the scope of my fears was so overwhelming that after my final stay at the Orthopedic Hospital, each night I continued to cover my head into my mid-twenties the same way I did while I was hospitalized.

So why did my parents put me into a situation that generated so much fear? I am positive they were doing what they thought was the best for me.

As an adult, I am delighted with the results from the four surgeries, but no one ever asked me if I wanted to spend my days and nights that added up to the better part of a year stuck in the boys ward. Or if I wanted to endure the pain from boiling hot wool strips, the agonizing muscle stretching, and four surgeries.

At a clinic visit the week before I returned to the Orthopedic Hospital for my fourth and final operation, Doctor Lowman explained to me that during this surgery, he would destroy the growth plates below the knee in my right leg so that, by the time I reached sixteen, both of my legs should be the same length.

That part of my visit with Doctor Lowman made me happy. From age five to eleven, I had worn a metal brace attached to my shoe with a built up heel and I was tired of the kids making fun of me. Every day at school, I wore my jeans as close to the ground as I could, so low they scraped the dirt, hoping no one would notice my brace and my fat left heel. After my third operation, I didn't need a brace anymore, but every recess, when we played Dodgeball or some other game, the captains always picked me last. Nobody wanted a kid on their team who couldn't run very fast.

All that was left was this operation and, in time, my left leg would be the same as my right and that meant no more fat heel.

During the thirty two weeks, approximately two hundred and twenty four days of my childhood I spent growing up in the third floor boys' ward at the Orthopedic Hospital, Juan was the only boy I met that I could call a friend. Some nights, after the lights went out, he and I would talk about what we were going to do when we grew up, but during my last stay, Juan was not there.

I did some research on living with hemophilia in the year 1951, when Juan would have been 13 or 14 years old, and discovered that he was long past the life expectancy of a child with that disease. Today, I can only assume that my hospital friend had died from his disease. And the truly sad part is that I had no way to find out because I never asked Juan's last name, nor he mine. Obviously, to a couple of lonely boys living in the third floor boys' ward, exchanging surnames was secondary to finding a friend.

The hospital routine in the boys' ward had not changed since my last surgery. Fourteen beds. Comic book delivery each Monday. No television. No radios. Actually, there was one change. The now teenaged Spaz was still trapped in his crib-like-bed, but the bars were taller.

By the time I reached thirteen, I had lived with the consequences of polio for eight years and now had a right hand with eighty percent of its normal strength, and a left foot that I could finally lift high enough that I could walk without a brace. When Dr. Lowman informed me that my final surgery was to be performed on my right leg, my GOOD leg, I was troubled. I had lived throughout my childhood with one good leg and one bad leg, so I had become very protective of my good leg. But Doctor Lowman convinced me to trust him and let him do the surgery on my good leg.

As usual, he was right. After the deed was done, I ended up with a cast from the top of my hip to my ankle. While I recovered in the hospital, my right leg floated three feet above the mattress, held there by an elevation device that lifted the foot of my bed.

My cast was long and heavy. I was then, and still am, a person who wants to fall asleep while lying on my stomach. There I was with my right leg stuck three feet in the air, trying to figure out, night after night, a way to get onto my stomach so I could fall asleep;. Finally, on the fifth night after the surgery, I turned my elevated right leg inside the sling and rolled onto my stomach. My right leg was still elevated, but upside down, and my cast was slightly askew, but still three feet off the mattress, and topped off with my left leg. I closed my eyes, hoped the night nurse wouldn't notice the change, and immediately fell asleep.

That first night I turned my leg, the night nurse woke me and wanted to know what I was doing. I explained that I was okay—that I had to fall asleep lying on my stomach. She told me that she was going to check with my doctor to be sure I wasn't doing some harm to my leg. I guess Doctor Lowman told her that what I was doing was okay, because she didn't bother me again.

As I look back, I imagine that I made a strange picture sleeping on my stomach with my blanket wrapped around my head and only my nose sticking out, and both legs turned upside down inside the traction device.

But worrying how I looked as I fell asleep was a minor problem compared to the major embarrassment that happened to me near the end of my hospital stay.

After more than two hundred days in the boys' ward, with nothing but a thin cloth curtain between my bed and everyone else, most would assume that I was inured to the nakedness, and reek of urine, and the noise and smell of bowel movements. But in fact, the exact opposite was true. I was, and still am, a very private person. For example, I close the door to the bathroom even when I am the only person at home.

Two days before I was to leave the Orthopedic Hospital for the last time, a nurse walked up to my bed and closed the privacy curtain around us. It was time for my sponge bath. But unlike all the other times I was given a sponge bath, this time the nurse was new and was very, very pretty. Thinking back, it was possible that a surge of hormones from a thirteen-year-old male made her seem prettier, but regardless of the reason, that sponge bath turned out to be the most embarrassing moment of my two hundred twenty-four days of hospital living.

First, you need to remember that I had a full length cast on my right leg and that my leg was elevated. Next, in case you don't know, a hospital sponge bath consists of someone else washing your body with a washcloth using warm, soapy water. Regular sponge baths are extremely important in a hospital setting, especially among those with limited mobility, where the inability to turn in bed may cause bedsores that can easily become infected. The rinsing aspect of the sponge bath is usually the most important and difficult part because you must rub the wet washcloth over the freshly washed skin more than once to pick up all the soapy residue. That's where my mortification began.

While the nurse rubbed the area between my legs with the wet washcloth to rinse off all the soap, I began to feel a warm glow in the pit of my stomach. As that warm feeling grew, so did my penis. I could sense, and see, what was happening. I tried to stop it from getting larger by looking at the ceiling, the floor, or by thinking about the whiner in the bed next to me. I wanted to get my mind onto anything but the pretty nurse. I tried desperately to picture something else, like playing baseball, or eating Halloween candy, or going home, or anything but what I was thinking, but once my locomotive got its steam up, it was going to do its best to leave the station.

Then, out of the corner of her eye, the pretty nurse saw my erection. She quickly tossed the washcloth in her right hand and deftly, with a flip of her wrist, snapped the tip of my penis with the damp washcloth.

That was a shock to both my libido and my erection, and my penis deflated faster than a rubber balloon that had been pierced with a pin.

Beyond her perfectly aimed snap of the washcloth, neither the nurse, nor I, ever acknowledged that anything unusual had happened and she completed my sponge bath without further incident.

After the nurse took the basin, washcloth, and soap off the bed, I was left lying there in some sort of an unfulfilled state. As I watched her leave, I decided that this sponge bath was going to be the last one of my life.

During my final days in the boys' ward, every time the pretty nurse walked into the ward, I grabbed my book and pretended to read. But when I peeked over the top of my book, I noticed that she seemed to avoid looking in my direction. Was it possible that my erection had embarrassed her more than it had me?

Seventy years after polio had altered my

life, one question still niggles at me: Why me? Why did the virus pick me, a helpless five-year-old boy? Was it because at age three and four I had been a very stubborn child? My mother told a story that one day, to get my way while she shopped for groceries, I held my breath so long that I passed out in the aisle. Today, I know that being obstinate had nothing to do with waking up one morning with polio, but my streak of stubbornness certainly helped me cope with my disease. Persistent, tenacious, dogged, and single-minded are a few positive synonyms of obstinate.

But my question remained unanswered. How did my brother and sister, or the other kids on my block escape polio? Was my paralysis the simple result of winning the poliovirus lottery?

Even today, sixty years after the release of the Salk vaccine, no one knows the exact answer to my question. Once the devastating polio epidemics came to a screeching halt, the March of Dimes stopped funding further research as to why some cases of polio caused paralysis or death, while others infected with the poliovirus exhibited nothing more than flu-like symptoms.

After talking with family members, interviewing medical professionals, and researching peer reviewed periodicals, newspapers, and a great many books on the subject of polio, I have finally come to the conclusion that I was just one of the unlucky ones. But unlucky or not, at some point in my life, I have accepted the simple truth that polio had significantly changed my future. Generally, polio changed my life in negative ways, but once in a while, the impact of polio turned out to be positive, and here is a perfect example of what I mean.

In August of 1951, after I left the Orthopedic Hospital for the last time, my right leg was incased in a full cast from my ankle to my hip. I couldn't bend my right knee and in a few weeks I was scheduled to return to Audubon Junior High School for my eighth grade year. During the seventh grade, I had never thought about the fact that the majority of the Audubon campus consisted of a large two-story building that required students to walk up and down the stairs to and from class. Nor had I foreseen that during my eighth grade, I would have to navigate those crowded stairs on crutches with a right leg that could not bend. In 1951, there were no laws, state or federal, that required any sort of accommodation for disabled people. In fact, all over America parents were informed that their local school districts would not, or could not, accommodate their children who had been disabled by polio.

Mom discussed my limited ability to climb stairs with the school administration at Audubon. They informed her that they were unable to help her figure out what to do with her temporarily disabled son.

But, here comes the serendipitous part. In 1951, my mom worked at a single story campus called Westchester Junior/Senior High School, a new school that had been constructed a few miles north of the Los Angeles International Airport. She asked the administration at Westchester for permission to enroll me as an out-of-district student for my eighth grade year. That is why I did not return to Audubon Junior High School in 1951.

Westchester Junior/Senior High School had been built during an interesting period in Los Angeles when the school system was having trouble keeping up with an unexpected growth of students. At Westchester, the district combined the junior and senior high schools into a single campus by running a double schedule. The senior high students started school at 7:45 am and finished at 12:15pm. The junior high students then started school at 12:45 and the school day was complete at 4:15.

Things worked out great for me because I could ride with my mom to school in the morning, do homework in the library and attend my classes until my mom was ready to go home around 4:30 or 5:00. After my cast was removed in November, I remained at Westchester and ultimately earned my High School diploma at that campus in June of 1956.

Why did I stay at Westchester when I

should have returned to Audubon for my ninth grade? Because for the first time in my life, I enjoyed going to school! The students at Westchester didn't know me or my history of braces and a built-up left shoe. Even though I spent part of my eighth grade year making my way around the campus on crutches before the cast on my right leg was removed, I was treated by the other kids more like an injured football player than that same crippled kid from elementary school.

During my high school years, I managed to remain at Westchester through some sort of bureaucratic error, but mistake or not, I liked attending that school and wanted to remain where I was. I didn't want to go back to Audubon and then Dorsey High to hear the same old crippled kid ridicule. So at the end of my eighth grade year, I didn't march into the principal's office, pound on her desk and demand a return to Audubon. It was as if the system depended on the out-of-boundry students to ask to return, rather than the administration keeping track of them.

Why do I feel that I slipped through an administrative crack? In 1956, with less than two months before my June graduation, I was walking to my next class, rounded the corner of a building and nearly crashed into the school registrar, the very woman in charge of keeping track of all the students at Westchester.

She stared at me for a moment and said,

"You're Ken Dalton, right?"

I said, "Yes."

"Are you still attending Westchester?"

"I am."

"But I thought . . . " She stopped, stood back and looked me up and down. "Ken, is this your senior Year?"

"Yes, it is."

She smiled. "Then I guess it's too late. Have a good graduation."

Going to to a different high school was good for me, but there was also a negative side to my attending an out-of-boundry school, a scenario that eluded me until I wrote this book.

While I attended Westchester High School, my sister and brother attended Dorsey High School. The gap between siblings, a tiny crack that began the day the ambulance rushed me to the Los Angeles County Hospital, continued to widen as we grew to become adults.

Throughout our formative high school years, we attended separate football games. During the school year, we danced at different proms and each day we socialized with a completely different group of friends.

Perhaps more important than our separate schools and social lives, both my brother and sister felt that their brother with polio always ended up with more than his share of our family's financial, parental love or nurturing resources.

I know there is no way to travel back in time to verify my supposition that my polio pushed us apart, but I still believe that even though my brother and sister had escaped the viral infection, the polio virus had a strong impact on their lives as well.

About a year before I returned to the Orthopedic Hospital for my final surgery, my family moved from our house on Orange Grove to a home in Baldwin Hills, a very nice area located in the southwest portion of Los Angeles. The day before I left the hospital, my mom and dad rented a hospital bed for me and rearranged the living room furniture to accommodate the large bed. After six weeks of Spartan life in the boys' ward, the living room in our new home seemed to me like a king's palace.

But getting to the palace was something else. Our new house was built on a hill with over two flights of stairs from the driveway to the living room. My dad and our neighbor, Mr. Calvert (a high school gym teacher with muscles on top of muscles who was always known as Mr. Calvert to the neighborhood boys), carried me, now a growing boy of thirteen, up those two flights. To make the effort even more difficult, there was a ninety degree right turn in the middle of the stairway. Judging by the grunts, groans and curses that spewed from my dad and Mr. Calvert, lifting me and my heavy, fully casted right leg through the tight turn had to be tough work. Their herculean effort remains with me as an unforgettable but scary memory.

The rented hospital bed in the living room was going to be my home for the next eight weeks and my life was great. Each morning my sister would turn the handle at the foot of the bed and the mattress part behind my head and shoulders would rise up so I could read or play games. If someone turned on the TV or the radio (no remotes back then), I could watch a show or listen to the afternoon Kids' shows on the radio.

The bed had wheels and could be rolled away from the wall so my mom could vacuum the carpet. Those wheels seemed like a great idea until one day the wheels provided me with an indelible impression that will live with me for the rest of my life.

First, everyone who does not live in a cave knows that California is the capital of earthquake country and that "the big one" could happen at any moment. But the earthquake that hit Los Angeles that summer day was not a "the big one." In fact, it was so small that looking back, I am sure the temblor did not reach 4.0 on the Richter Scale.

At that point in my recuperation, I was not supposed to crawl, much less walk and then the earthquake struck. Suddenly I was trapped on a bed that rolled and bounced around our living room. With visions of the house breaking away from its foundation and sending the bed, with me on it, shooting down steep Marburn Avenue, I grabbed the sides of the mattress and held on for what looked like the last wild ride of my life.

A moment after the quake began, the earth stopped shaking and so did the bed. Both my mom and dad were at work, so it was my sister and brother who ran into the living room to see if I was okay. We were all surprised to find the head of the bed had spun one hundred and eighty degrees. After Pat and Richard turned my bed back around, I asked Pat to turn on the TV and we all watched Queen for a Day to settle our frayed nerves.

To this day, I can close my eyes and see myself panic stricken, holding the sides of the mattress and riding the bed around the living room like I was a rodeo cowboy atop a crazed brahma bull.

With my right leg was incased in the plaster cast that ran from my ankle to the top of my hip, I was not allowed to put any weight on my right leg for a month after I left the hospital, but that was not the part that bugged me the most. While I was still in the hospital. But that was not the post surgery part that bugged me the most. Dr. Lowman told my mom he was concerned that during the next few months of my forced sedentary life, I had the potential to gain weight, so he gave my mom a list of low calorie foods and told her that I should ingest no more than 1200 calories a day!

Every day, my mom cooked the family breakfast and dinner. Because my food was different, I ate all my meals alone in my bed in the living room so I would not have to see or smell what everyone else was eating and get envious.

As close as I can recall, the 1200 calorie a day restriction was not bad, but it wasn't good either. The biggest drawback was not the lack of bacon or ice cream, it was the loss of my self-esteem. Over the previous eight years of my life, I had learned to cope with wearing a brace attached to a shoe with a three inch heel, pooping into a bedpan, and being picked last for the kickball team during recess, but for some unknown reason, being called fat was the straw that broke the camel's back. During the following weeks, I hardly touched the food my mom prepared and the next time I saw Dr. Lowman, I asked him if I could go off the 1200 calorie a day diet. He stood back, looked me up and down, and declared I was fit, not fat. To my joy, he told my mom that she could stop the diet.

That was good news, but the fear of being perceived as being fat, or even tending toward a few extra pounds, has remained in the back of my mind throughout my life.

So what did I do while I was stuck in bed in the living room, besides staring at a bunch of quiz shows or soap operas on TV? Or waiting until the late afternoon when Jack Armstrong, Sergeant Preston of the Mounted Police, or Sky King come on the radio?

I played games with Bill and Mel, a couple of guys who lived on Marburn Avenue. Bill's house was directly across from our new home and Mel lived two doors down the hill. After I returned from my hospital stay, they would came over and play cards or board games with me.

Having the hospital bed at home gave me the opportunity to be with my friends, but after a while, even cards or Monopoly got old. But playing the Cadaco All Star Baseball game with my buddy Mel was never boring and remains one of my fondest memories of the summer of 1951.

Mel and I were both baseball fans, and as crazy as it sounds, the game made me feel like we were really playing baseball in my living room. How was that possible? The game consisted of a spinner attached to a cardboard square and a bunch of round cards with a rectangular cutout in the middle that allowed the cards to fit on the spinner square. Each card had the name of a real major league baseball player and, here is the important part, had fourteen number segments of varying widths printed on the face of the cards. The width of the lines that separated the segments actually corresponded to the batting statistics for each individual player.

For example, Babe Ruth's card had a giant number one segment at the top of his card. The width of the number one segment equated to the Babe's prodigious ability to hit home runs. The home run segment measured more than an inch wide, but the width of Ruth's giant number one segment was correct because he had hit 714 home runs in 8,399 at bats. The opposite example to Babe Ruth's card would be the card for Richie Ashburn. Richie played for the Phillies and he seldom hit a home run. With only twenty nine home runs in 8,368 at bats, Ashburn's number one segment was only 1/8 of an inch wide.

But how could a stack of round cards and a spinner make two boys feel like they were playing baseball?

Using Babe Ruth's card as an example, I would place the Babe's card on the spinner square, flick the tip of the arrow with my finger, and the arrow would spin around and around. Wherever the pointer of the arrow stopped, that would be Babe's turn at bat. If the pointer landed on number one, Babe would have hit a home run. If it landed on a ten, Babe would strike out. If the pointer landed on a thirteen, Babe would get a single.

When my team was up at bat, I would go through each player on my team until my team scored three outs. Then it would be Mel's turn with his team and their cards. After nine innings, as long as the score wasn't tied, our game would be over.

The day we opened the All Star Baseball game box, each of us picked nine players and those players comprised a team. But one team was not enough for us. Mel and I each had four teams that played against each other—the National League because Mel was a Brooklyn Dodger fan against the American League because I was a Micky Mantle fan and that sort of made me a New York Yankee fan.

Once our schedule of games were finished for the day and Mel went home, that was when my real job started. I had a book where I kept the batting statistics for each player plus the win and loss records for each team.

Toward the end of my recuperation, we finished our planned baseball season with a best out of seven "World Series" finale.

Those days Mel and I spent playing All Star Baseball were great and keeping track of the seventy two players' batting statistics took up a lot of my down time, something all patients stuck in a bed had to deal with.
After I finished writing the story of my summer playing All Star Baseball with Mel, on a whim, I went on line to Ebay and was surprised to find out that All Star Baseball is still being played with new cards representing the batting statistics of many modern day players. I also

chuckled when I spotted a used 1950s Cadaco All Star Baseball board game going for a cool $180.00. Wow! I wonder if there's a chance that my old game board is still tucked away somewhere in someone's closet.

In Dr. Sabin's obituary, there was the following quote from Dr. Salk: "Albert Sabin was out for me from the very beginning. I remember in Copenhagen in 1960, he said to me, just like that, that he was out to kill the killed vaccine."
The Albert Sabin Obituary-New Your Times-March 4, 1993

In Dr. Salk's obituary, there was the following quote from Dr. Sabin made prior to Sabin's death: "It was pure kitchen chemistry. Salk didn't discover anything."
The Jonas Salk Obituary-New York Times-June 24, 1995

CHAPTER SEVENTEEN

1954—Salk Wins the Polio Vaccine Race

Once Enders and his team proved that the polio virus could be propagated in non-nervous tissue, scientists throughout the world jumped into the frantic race to produce the first polio vaccine.

Among those who succeeded in producing a viable vaccine were Dr. Jonas Salk, who used dead polio virus, and Dr. Albert Sabin, Dr. Hilary Koprowski, and Herald R. Cox, Sc.D., who used live, but attenuated (weakened) polio virus.

Today, nearly everyone has heard of Dr.

Salk and Dr. Sabin, but who were Hilary Koprowski and Herald Cox, and how did they miss grabbing the brass ring?

Hilary Koprowski was born in Warsaw, Poland, on Dec. 5, 1916. He simultaneously attended the Warsaw Music Conservatory where he received a music degree and Warsaw University where he earned his medical degree in 1939.

Later that year, after the German invasion of Poland, Dr. Koprowski, who was of Jewish extraction, left the country with his family. He ended up in Rome where he continued his music studies and then moved to Rio de Janeiro, where he worked on a yellow fever project for the Rockefeller Foundation. In 1944, Dr. Koprowski arrived in the United States and worked for Herald Cox, Sc.D., who led the prestigious Lederle Laboratories.

Dr. Koprowski was a leading biomedical researcher and helped to develop many innovations, including a safer, less painful, and more effective rabies vaccine that remains widely used today.

In 1950, while working under Cox at Lederle Lab, he developed the first successful polio vaccine four years before Salk's initial vaccine trial.

Koprowski attenuated his polio virus by repeatedly injecting it into the brain tissue of the cotton rat, a rare genus that was susceptible to polio. Koprowski theorized that as the virus became comfortable living in the rodent's brain, it would become less capable of growing or reproducing itself in people. To prove his theory he tossed a dozen cotton rats' brains into a blender, and downed the greasy, gray liquid himself.

The results? Beyond complaining that the weird concoction tasted like cod liver oil, Koprowski had successfully inoculated himself against polio—years before the vaccines of Salk or Sabin became available.

Flushed with visions of developing the first polio vaccine, Koprowski took a risk and convinced Gregory Dick, a highly respected virologist from Great Britain, to run a trial of his live, attenuated polio vaccine on two hundred volunteers in Belfast, Ireland. The risk? If the live virus had not been attenuated (weakened) enough, it could become virulent (effective) and cause polio, the very disease the vaccine was attempting to prevent.

Dick initially agreed, but during the Belfast trial, he was shocked to discover that some of Koprowski's vaccine had become virulent as it traveled through the intestinal tract of the two hundred volunteers, a group that included Dick's four-year-old daughter, and some of the volunteers contracted polio. Gregory Dick immediately contacted Koprowski and demanded he stop the Belfast trial.

But Koprowski, with all the boldness of a cornered swashbuckler, accused Dick of hyperbole and reminded him that in all trials, there was always a price to be paid for advancements in the field of medicine.

I realize that I am jumping ahead of the story, but a final note on the Belfast trial: In 1962, based on his negative experience with Koprowski's vaccine that used live, attenuated viruses, Gregory Dick argued against his government's decision to replace the proven Salk vaccine with Sabin's live, attenuated oral vaccine.

Years later, after Salk's vaccine had been released for use on the general public, Koprowski ran a larger trial of his vaccine in the Belgian Congo but the results of that trial were inconclusive. Among the scientific community, there was no doubt that the Koprowski vaccine did cause some recipients to become infected with polio. Although Koprowski's vaccine was eventually given to patients overseas with some good results, his vaccine was never approved for use in the United States.

That takes us to Herald Cox. He was born in 1907 in Terre Haute, Indiana and graduated from Indiana State Normal School, now known as Indiana State University. In 1928, he obtained his doctorate from the Johns Hopkins Bloomberg School of Public Health. In the 1930s, Cox joined the U. S. Public Health Service and, as the Principal Bacteriologist at the Rocky Mountain Laboratory in Hamilton, Montana, he made discoveries that led to vaccines to fight Rocky Mountain spotted fever and several strains of typhus.

During 1942, Cox moved to New York where he became the head of the Virus and Rickettsial Research Department at the Lederle Laboratories, a division of American Cyanimid Company.

In October 1952, Cox reported that he was the first to grow the Lansing strain of the polio virus in fertile hens' eggs. In 1961, Cox finally announced he had developed an oral polio vaccine, but he was too late. The 1957 field trials of Sabin's oral vaccine had proved successful and Sabin's vaccine was licensed for general use in 1961.

A closing note concerning Koprowski and Cox. Sabin's successful polio vaccine was developed from an attenuated polio virus strain that he had received from Hilary Koprowski while Koprowski worked for Herald Cox at the Lederle Lab.

Initially, Sabin and Koprowski had supported each other during their attempts to develop an attenuated vaccine, but once Sabin had his vaccine, he rebuffed further requests from Koprowski to collaborate.

And while Sabin and Koprowski had worked together, Cox labored alone. In fact, he was forced to compete against his subordinate, Koprowski. But for his years of labor, all Cox managed to accomplish was to develop the *last* successful attenuated vaccine, four years after Sabin had already won the race.

Both Koprowski and Cox came agonizingly close to achieving the desired title of polio's conqueror, but each just missed his moment of fame.

Having developed a workable vaccine ahead of Koprowski and Cox, Salk and Sabin battled it out to see who could produce the first, safest, and most effective version of the polio vaccine.

The truly strange part of the Salk and Sabin story is that they both came up with a relatively safe and effective polio vaccine, but there was a major and very important difference between the two vaccines. Dr. Salk used a dead virus, killed by employing a solution of water and formaldehyde (formalin). Dr. Sabin, on the other hand, used a live, attenuated strain of polio virus whose virulence had been lowered using chemical processes, or by repeated passage through the cells of another species. Vaccines made by using attenuated strains of live virus had prevented smallpox, measles, mumps, rubella, and yellow fever. And the great majority of researchers believed that an attenuated virus was the preferred medium when compared to the killed virus, and would produce the safest, and most successful vaccines.

So there were major differences between

the vaccines, but there were also major differences between the two researchers.

Salk was eight years younger than Sabin, a salient point that the elder researcher never let Salk forget.

Salk, in the opinion of the majority of the scientific community, was an upstart publicity seeker, whereas Sabin, old enough to have lived through Maurice Brodie's and John Kollmer's disastrous polio vaccines in the mid-thirties, and Flexner's "protect the nose and prevent polio" trial fiascos toward the end of the thirties, followed a more conservative approach to publicity.

Funded by the NFIP, Salk, Sabin, and other researchers, worked together during the 1949 effort to determine how many types of polio viruses existed. Altogether, the team spent $1,200,000, sacrificed more than 17,000 monkeys, and met occasionally to discuss progress. During one of those meetings, Salk was mortified when Sabin berated him in front of his research peers, taking him to task over some point of discussion by proclaiming, "Dr. Salk, you should know better than to ask a question like that."

From the moment of Sabin's demeaning comment, Salk decided that he and Sabin would never again collaborate on any research, much less work together to create a polio vaccine.

Salk and Sabin were decidedly mortal with

all the usual human frailties such as giant egos, stubbornness, and the capacity to carry a grudge to the grave, but their individual successes gave them both membership into the scientific pantheon of polio heroes, on a par with the Greek gods who occupy Mount Olympus.

Dr. Jonas Salk was born in 1914, grew up in New York city, and entered City College of New York at age fifteen. After graduating from medical school in 1939, Salk determined that he wanted to use his medical degree to do research rather than practice medicine, and he immediately joined an army-commissioned project to develop an influenza vaccine. Salk, working with Dr. Thomas Francis, Jr., spent four years working on the influenza virus. The vaccine that they developed in 1943 used a killed influenza virus that would not cause the disease but did induce antibodies able to ward off future viral attacks. Francis and Salk were among the pioneers of the killed-virus concept. Up to then, attenuated live viruses had been used to produce vaccines.

In 1948, Salk established a research lab as an adjunct to the University of Pittsburgh School of Medicine where he undertook the project to determine the number of different types of polio virus. In addition to his brilliant research capability, Salk was an astute businessman. He immediately recognized the initial NFIP funding as an opportunity to develop a closer relationship with the charitable organization to fund more research on developing a polio vaccine. For the next seven years, Salk focused the skilled research team he had assembled toward the goal of a successful polio vaccine.

One of Salk's first decisions was to choose what type of vaccine he would attempt to produce, an attenuated live virus or a killed virus. Salk's previous work on his influenza vaccine led him to theorize that a polio vaccine that used the killed virus could produce a safer and effective vaccine.

In 1953, after Salk had performed limited trials on small groups of children, he reported his positive results to the NFIP Committee on Polio Vaccines. It may have been the fact that the country had just come through the worst polio summer on record (more than 50,000 new cases), but the committee ignored the negative arguments of Sabin and other researchers, and backed Salk's vaccine. One year later, a massive field trial, the magnitude of which has not been seen before or since, was organized to test Salk's vaccine. In the spring of 1954, he launched an enormous, nationwide trial with more than 2,200,000 children at a cost of $5,000,000.

As we all know, nothing in life comes easily. There was disagreement as to how the field trial should be conducted. One plan, backed by the NFIP, proposed to offer vaccinations to second graders at participating schools and compare the results with the non-vaccinated first and third graders at the same school. This is known in the research world as the observed-control approach.

But many scientists objected to the observed-control approach and suggested using a true double-blind trial where half of the participants would be given the actual vaccine while the other half would be injected with a saline solution placebo. This is know as the placebo-control approach.

Eventually, both trial methods were used with 750,000 participating in the placebo-control trial and over a 1,000,000 children in the observed-control trial.

Over the following twelve months, a manual record was created for each of the more than two million participants. With no financial support from the Federal government or pharmaceutical companies, and decades before easier data collection methods became available through the invention of computers, the bulk of the results of Salk's 1954 trial were edited and coded using pencil and paper by dozens of Michigan graduate students who were paid $1.25 an hour by the NFIP.

On April 12, 1955, twelve months after Salk's huge field trials began, and more than forty years after Dr. Simon Flexner's premature promise of a polio vaccine, the news of the successful polio vaccine was made public.

Although the vaccine was not one hundred percent effective, those vaccinated were less than one-half as likely to contract polio as the non-vaccinated control groups.

Salk's vaccine was declared a triumph and he was hailed as a miracle worker. After the 1954 trial proved the efficacy of Salk's vaccine, the federal government licensed Cutter Laboratories, along with several other pharmaceutical firms, to produce the Salk vaccine. The United States, Canada, and most of the countries in Europe immediately started polio immunization campaigns using the newly produced Salk vaccine. Unfortunately at Cutter Laboratories, something went awry during the production of the vaccine and that mistake created the event know as the Cutter Incident.

The Cutter Labs accidentally produced 120,000 doses of the polio vaccine that contained live polio virus! Of the children who received the potentially deadly vaccine, one-third developed a mild form of polio, an infection that did not invade the central nervous system, but fifty-six developed paralytic polio and five of those children died. Further, the person-to-person exposure to the polio virus in the communities where the 40,000 affected children lived also led to a mini-polio epidemic that resulted in an additional 113 paralyzed victims and five more deaths.

An immediate investigation showed that the National Institute of Health (NIH)

Laboratory of Biologics Control, which had certified the Cutter polio vaccine, had received an advance warning in 1954 that all viruses were not dead. This alert came when a staff member at Cutter Labs, Dr. Bernice Eddy, reported to her superiors that some inoculated monkeys (animals used to validate the safety of the produced vaccine) had become paralyzed and that the vaccine was potentially harmful to recipients.

For reasons that remain unknown today, William Sebrell, the Director of NIH, either never saw or ignored Dr. Eddy's warning that the Cutter polio vaccine contained live viruses and could cause polio.

After the incident, Surgeon General Leonard Scheele sent Drs. William Tripp and Karl Habel from the NIH to inspect Cutter's facilities in Berkeley, California where they questioned workers and examined records. After a thorough investigation, the two found nothing wrong with Cutter's production methods. A Congressional hearing on the Cutter Incident in June 1955 concluded that the problem was primarily due to the lack of scrutiny from the NIH's Laboratory of Biologics Control.

A number of civil lawsuits were filed against Cutter Laboratories in subsequent years. The first suit was Gottsdanker v. Cutter. The jury found that Cutter was not negligent, but that it was liable for breach of implied warranty, and awarded the plaintiffs monetary damages. That trial set a precedent for later lawsuits. All five companies that produced the Salk vaccine in 1955—Eli Lilly, Parke-Davis, Wyeth, Pitman-Moore, and Cutter—reported having some difficulty totally inactivating the polio virus. Three additional pharmaceutical companies were sued, and those cases were settled out of court. The Cutter incident turned out to be one of the worst pharmaceutical disasters in the United States, and in its aftermath, the Director of the NIH Laboratory of Biologics Control lost his job. The Assistant Secretary for Health, Oveta Culp Hobby, stepped down, and Dr. William Sebrell, the Director of the NIH, resigned.

The last scientist in the race to develop a successful polio vaccine was Dr. Albert Sabin. He was born in 1906, in Bialystok, Poland, to Jacob and Tillie Saperstein, and emigrated with his parents to America in 1922. In 1930, he attended New York University, became a naturalized citizen of the United States ,and changed his name to Sabin. In 1931, Sabin received his medical degree and began his research career at the Rockefeller Institute.

In the early 1950s, like many scientists of the time, Sabin believed that only a living virus would be able to guarantee immunity for an extended period and he therefore developed an attenuated live virus vaccine that could be administered orally. The first trial of his oral vaccine was tested on children at the Chillicothe, Ohio Reformatory in late 1954.

By the time Sabin's polio vaccine was ready for large field trials, Salk's polio vaccine was already being administered to millions of Americans. Between 1955 and 1961, Sabin took his oral vaccine to the USSR, where it was successfully tested on over 100 million people.

In 1958, faced with three competing live virus vaccines, the National Institute of Health (NIH) created a special committee to evaluate the researchers' work. The, Koprowski, Cox, and Sabin vaccines were carefully analyzed for their ability to safely induce immunity to polio while retaining a low incidence of pathological changes to a monkeys nervous system. Based on the NIH evaluation and the results of world-wide trials, the Sabin live virus strain was chosen for worldwide distribution.

Finally, the battle lines between Salk's and Sabin's vaccines were drawn:

The Salk vaccine was administered through injection.

The Sabin vaccine was administered through drops on a sugar cube.

The Salk vaccine was produced from a killed virus.

The Sabin vaccine was produced from a live, but attenuated virus.

The Salk vaccine could require booster shots.

The Sabin single sugar cube of vaccine

could provide lifetime immunity.

Rapidly, the Sabin vaccine, based on its lower cost, ease of use, and with the potential of lifetime immunity, became the vaccine of choice in the United States and other countries throughout the world.

But, after nearly two decades of distribution throughout the world, an important defect with the Sabin vaccine materialized. Sabin's vaccine actually caused polio in one out of every 2,400,000 doses.

On October 20, 1998, after eighteen years of the exclusive use of the Sabin vaccine in the United States, the CDC recommended that all children would be inoculated against polio using the Salk vaccine. Since that time, Sabin's polio vaccine has not been available in the United States.

If questioned about the competitive doctors, most scientists refused to take sides in the Salk versus Sabin battle. I found no criticism concerning Sabin, but Salk was another story. Many felt that Salk had alienated himself from the scientific community by forming too close a relationship with the NFIP. Fellow researchers were also uncomfortable with Salk's use of a killed virus since the majority firmly believed that using an attenuated virus vaccine was the only proven way to make a safe vaccine. Finally, in the race to be the first to produce a polio vaccine, Salk did the unthinkable when he did not submit his research for peer review, the standard protocol in the scientific world.

After 1998, Sabin's vaccines continued to be used in countries with hard-to-reach communities. Those countries decided that an infection rate of 1 out of every 2.4 million doses was a major improvement when compared to having thousands and thousands of their citizens stricken each year during their annual polio epidemics. Even today, the fear of continued polio epidemics overshadows the guaranteed polio rate of 1 out of 2.4 million vaccine recipients.

But the battle lines were drawn and the two doctors were ready to fight dirty if needed.

According to his son, Salk was a very private person, but during a 1977 Canadian Broadcasting Company TV interview, Salk offered this thinly veiled attack against Sabin and his vaccine: "In spite of the evidence at the time that the killed virus vaccine (his) was doing all the things that they said it wasn't doing, and the assertion that the live virus vaccine (Sabin's) could be given without risk of paralysis when all of us knew that (polio) cases had been occurring in countries where it (Sabin's) had been used."

So which man eventually won the battle of the vaccines? It truly does not matter because Salk's killed vaccine effectively stopped the polio epidemics in the United States. And Sabin's live, attenuated vaccine, administered through some drops of the vaccine on a sugar cube, proved to be the most effective way to reach hundreds of millions of unvaccinated men, women, and children throughout the world.

Despite the differences between the competing vaccines, polio cases in the United States dropped from a pre-vaccine high of 58,000 reported cases in 1952, to 121 cases reported in 1964. Today, polio is an unknown disease in the United States.

Finally, it is important to realize that neither man sought to patent his vaccine, demonstrating that both men made their vaccines for the benefit of mankind, not for profit. It has been estimated that if Salk and Sabin had been granted patents, those patents would have generated an approximate 2.5 billion dollar payday for Salk, and 6 billion dollars for Sabin.

It is also interesting to note that neither Salk nor Sabin was ever awarded a Nobel prize for their vaccine discoveries. As I wrote at the end of Chapter Seven, that honor, the Nobel Prize for Physiology or Medicine in 1954, was presented to John F. Enders, Thomas H. Weller, and Fredrick C. Robbins, for their breakthrough discovery that proved the polio virus could be grown on non-nervous tissue.

Salk and Sabin continued their work through long careers. Dr. Salk opened The Salk Institute for Biological Studies in the 1960s with the following motto: "Jonas Salk knew there was more to conquer than polio. So he built an institute to do it."

The Sabin Vaccine Institute was founded in 1993 after the death of Dr. Albert B. Sabin. The Institute annually awards the Albert B. Sabin Gold Medal in recognition of outstanding achievement in the field of vaccinology.

Salk and Sabin certainly possessed oversized egos but that may have been what was required to accomplish what had not been done before.

They may not have ever gotten along, or even liked each other, but together those two men changed the world as their vaccines saved millions, and all future generations to come, from paralysis or death.

When polio patients finally returned home, many of them faced a difficult period of adjustment. They were not the same persons physically, emotionally, or psychologically. Accommodations had to be made for the remaining disabilities and assistive devices. Other family members sometimes resented the extra attention paid to the polio survivor.
***Living With Polio,* Daniel J. Wilson**

CHAPTER EIGHTEEN

Families, Siblings, Parents, And Vacations

When I began this memoir, I thought that I understood, in general, what I was going to write about. However, the longer and deeper I dug into the memories, letters, and conversations with parents, siblings, and relatives, I realized, for the first time, that my eleven year journey had profoundly altered my understanding of what a family could and should be.

But what should I have expected?

Children develop their family expectations from their daily experiences through the process of gradual or unconscious assimilation of ideas and knowledge, the same way a child learns the native language of his or her parents.

In other words, a boy who lives in a home where his father barges in the front door roaring drunk after work, or whose mother dons a Brunhilda helmet and sings operatic arias as she irons the wrinkles out of her newly washed sheets, or an older sibling who sneaks into the closet to smoke a cigarette when his parents are not looking, could likely assume that all families include a drunken father, a crazy mother, and a sneaky sibling.

What was life in my family like prior to my illness in 1943? Well, we did not own a television set, a computer, nor did my mom and sister cruise the local shopping mall on the weekends, because, televisions, computers, and shopping malls did not exist. My parents carried no credit cards. We children had no video games. With little discretionary money to spend, there were very few family outings, even to the movies.

Each evening, once the dinner dishes were washed, dried, and put away, my family would sit in the living room and listen to The Ozzie and Harriet Show, or The Cisco Kid, or Fibber McGee and Molly, on the radio.

In the fall, on Saturday afternoons, I recall sitting on our living room floor with my dad and listening to UCLA football games. In his opinion, UCLA was the only Los Angeles area college team worth listening to, although I am pretty sure that my golf partner and USC grad, Walt Hale, would disagree with that biased opinion. My dad took the time to show me, using a pad of paper and a pencil, how to track UCLA's movements, up and down the field, during the football game. This was sort of like watching a football game on TV without a TV. We would also listen to an occasional baseball game where he taught me how to keep track of hits, errors, runs scored, and the RBIs of each Los Angeles Angels player.

I have no idea of the turmoil that went on in my household during my stay in the Contagion Building at the Los Angeles County Hospital, but within a week after I returned home, my dad was drafted into the army, and that changed expectations in a different way.

So here is how my family looked to me, a sick five-year-old boy, at that point: No father. A mother who spent most of her days wrapping me with wool strips for the Sister Kenny treatment method, and a brother and sister who had to feel as if they had lost both parents.

Recently, my brother sent me a copy of an email exchange he had with my sister, a few years before she died about growing up:

Richard (my younger brother) in an email to our sister, Pat stated—"I find it hard to explain my feelings about Mom and Pop without sounding like a callous rat. My reaction to all this was that there wasn't much I could count on at home so I'd just do without and get on with the job of raising myself."

Pat (my older sister) in an email to

Richard—"I could have written those lines."

My brother concluded his email to Pat—"When Mom went to visit Ken, you wound up being the default babysitter and we were relegated to the grassy area in front of the hospital . . . During her visits, Mom would hoist Ken up to his third floor window, where he could wave and give us a grin . . . that was the way of life for the next eleven years: Ken and Mom bound together by polio and you and I looking in."

Pat, died from chronic obstructive pulmonary disease (COPD) a few years before I started this book so I called her oldest daughter and asked if her mom had ever told her of any childhood problems caused by my polio. She said, "Mom's life was definitely affected, because Grandma Dalton was so focused on getting the best possible care for you that at times, Pat felt unseen, especially during the summers."

To put it mildly, my brother's, sister's, and niece's input were a shock to me.

Their revelations caused me to ask myself how I could have been so oblivious to the effect of my illness on my family.

After pondering my lack of understanding, I concluded that during the years of my hospitalizations, operations, and rehabilitation, I had developed a sort of tunnel vision, a goal passed on to me from Doctor Lowman—to be able to walk with a normal gait by the time I reached sixteen—and anything outside my tunnel vision did not exist.

As the kid who had polio, I know that those eleven years took all of my focus, but to learn, sixty-five years after the fact, that my illness had caused my sister and brother, major problems during their early years was unsettling to say the least.

And what about my mom and dad? Did my polio contribute to the failure of their marriage?

Today, I have no way of answering that question. My polio, combined with the social and economic differences that existed prior to their marriage, the empowerment of women during World War Two, and my dad's absence during the war, likely created the seeds of separation that grew into their divorce some time later. Regardless, I do understand that my mom and dad were not the only couple to divorce in the decade after World War Two.

A family story from my brother highlights the major social and economic differences between my parents:

"Our dad started off the marriage with two dozen pairs of socks. After he had worn them all, he saw that none of them had been washed, so he wore them again. Finally, faced with the third sock cycle, he asked my mom when she was going to do the laundry. Mom seemed nonplussed by the question, having never realized that doing the washing was her job."

Regardless of the reason, or reasons, I do

know this fact: by the time I had reached the age of sixteen, my parents were divorced.

I also know that my summer surgeries interrupted many potential family vacations. Family outings may seem like a trivial item, but in this case, I think the point my niece made about my sister feeling unseen, especially in the summers, is relevant.

Summer, when school is out, is the time most families get together and take a vacation. Remember that children learn about their family structure, and that of other families, by absorbing their surroundings.

Most of my friends in the neighborhood went on annual family vacations.

My wife's family took summer vacations nearly every year.

Her brother, Norm, with his wife, and children went on family vacations.

In my teens, I went on trips to the mountains where I camped and fished, but that was with the YMCA, not my family.

From 1943 to 1954, World War Two and my operations created roadblocks to Dalton family outings. For some reason my mom and dad never came up with a plan for a yearly vacation. Not a half-day road trip up the California coast to Santa Barbara. Or a two-hour drive to the mountains at Big Bear Lake. Or even a short drive to Balboa island for some family time at the beach.

Family vacations are valuable because

they offer the family the opportunity to develop a togetherness that can be difficult to find time for during the rest of the year. Vacations encourage the family to work together while discussing road trips, or camping, or the size of a rental cabin at the beach, or where to go in the mountains.

When I was twelve my parents attempted exactly one family vacation. My dad rented a cabin at Bass Lake from a fellow worker at the post office. After a half-day drive we arrived at the cabin, but before we finished unpacking the car, my mom made sure we all knew that the cabin was too small, or too old, and was located much too far from the lake. To this day I do not know the reason for my mom's ill temper, but the week at Bass Lake was the last time our family attempted a summer vacation.

Two years later, my neighborhood friend, Mel, and his family, invited me to go with them for a week camping at, you guessed it, Bass Lake. From the first day of the vacation, I noticed a totally different relationship between Mel's mom and dad. While I was present they never bickered, and they seemed to truly enjoy having their children and me around them for the whole week.

After my final operation in the summer of 1953, the last opportunity for my family to unite around something passed, and the decades-old infrastructure that had held my mom and dad's marriage together, the Gorilla glue so to speak, had lost its ability to bond and they divorced.

Another point to be made on family expectations.

After my wife and I were married, we consciously worked to develop a solid family bond with our children. Over forty years ago we moved from Los Angeles to Sonoma County so our family would have the opportunity to grow up in a rural atmosphere. And because my wife stayed home with our children, the lack of discretionary funds made being together easier. But as our children grew older, and money became easier, we still enjoyed our times with each other.

Nearly every year we vacationed together, including one camping trip for the whole family to Europe. We attended our children's back-to-school nights. My son played Little League baseball and I helped with the team. Our daughters were both Camp Fire Girls and Arlene was their leader.

We worked together on our three and a half acres in Sebastopol, picking apples and raised cows, pigs, and chickens. One day, after repairing a section of fence that had been crushed when a large tree limb fell, my son Hugh and I were walking up the hill to our home. Hugh was around age thirteen at the time and he remarked, "You know, Dad, we're getting pretty good at fixing fences."

My son's upbeat comment glows in my

memory as proof that we had created a family that lived, worked, and had fun together.

During our years in Sebastopol we were also privileged to have had two exchange students live with us for the better part of a year; Eva, came from Sweden, and two years later, Tanja, arrived from Germany. We still keep in contact through emails to each other on a regular basis. And we still get together, either in America, or Europe. One evening, while eating dinner, Tanja, who at that point had lived with us for only two to three weeks, burst into tears and wanted to know when we were going to stop pretending with our happy-family charade. For a moment I was nonplussed, and then I told Tanja that we were not pretending. Until her outburst, I had not realized that Arlene and I had accomplished our goal of creating the family that polio had taken away.

If polio eradication is a 20th-century dream, conceived by idealists and driven by big international institutions and volunteers, it must succeed or fail in a century marked by factionalism, religious intolerance and rising inequality. It may have taken an outbreak of an even more terrifying disease, Ebola, to demonstrate the crucial role of eradicating a disease of the past.
***Newsweek*, Karen Bartlett, November, 28, 2014**

EPILOGUE

So there you have it. My journey with polio, from waking one morning with a fever when I was five, to a hand-shake with Dr. Lowman, to walking with a normal gait at sixteen, to building a fine life beyond my illness.

I spent eleven years of my life, endured four operations, and endless physical therapy sessions, all so I could walk like everyone else. Today, after more than sixty years have passed, I still walk with a normal gait. But I learned that walking like everyone else took some conscious effort on my part. Over time, that conscious effort became unconscious, and almost no one, except my family, would know that I had polio as a child.

By the time I was in my mid-twenties, if I went through a physically demanding week at work, a colleague might ask me, “Ken, why are you limping?"

"It's just an old war wound," I would joke. Then I would remind myself that I needed to walk properly and my limp would again disappear.

As I grew older, walking with a normal gait was not my only goal. I felt the need to make up for my lost childhood, all those years I had missed playing baseball, basketball, and football, so running and playing sports became my mantra.

In high school I was a member of the swim team. My two events were breaststroke and individual medley. I was not a great swimmer, but good enough to earn my letter. Another perk, I passed geometry because the swim coach, Mr. Pollock, taught that class and he needed a good individual medley swimmer. I'm not proud of scooting through that math requirement, but Coach Pollock also taught algebra, and for some weird reason, I aced algebra.

My other brush with sports during high school was with the basketball team. I never tried out for the team because my mom would not give me the required permission, so I became a basketball team manager with my friend and fellow manager, John Yee.

Our job consisted of attending each practice, making sure the basketballs were handed out to team members, and picking up the balls after each practice. Truthfully, John and I spent most of our time learning how to shoot layups, hook shots, and jump shots. Coach Rankin knew I wanted to play, and that my mom would not give me her permission, so when his coaching time permitted, he would work with me on my shooting techniques.

By the time I reached my third decade, I finally had the chance to realize my childhood dream and played second base with a real softball team. I never mentioned to my other team members that I had never played softball, much less second base, but after successfully fielding a couple hundred balls during practice, and turning my first double play during a game, no one seemed to care about my lack of experience.

At forty, I played basketball with a team made up of phone company employees and quickly accepted what I already knew, that I was too short to get many rebounds but was much quicker than many of the tall guys. So I used my speed and became proficient at stealing the opponent's ball, sprinting down the court, and scoring two points with a lay up. Again, as with my softball team, none of my basketball team members were ever aware that I had never played basketball in an organized league.

As I blithely cruised into my sixties, more than fifty years had slipped by since my final "good leg" shortening surgery, and the residual effect from my childhood illness on my adult life was insignificant. But, as I approached my seventies, I became painfully aware of my advancing age. I began to wonder if I had post-polio syndrome (PPS), a condition that affects more than fifty percent of polio survivors, many, many years after they thought they had recovered from the illness.

PPS presents itself to polio survivors in areas previously affected by the polio virus when they notice progressive muscle weakness, fatigue, and an increase in muscle atrophy, along with pain from joint degeneration. While PPS is rarely a life-threatening condition, the symptoms can significantly interfere with an individual's ability to function independently.

Though I know this sounds ridiculous, I have to admit that the more I learned about PPS, the more irritated I became. Hundreds of thousands of polio survivors, people like myself who struggled through a childhood burdened by years of surgeries and physical therapy, were now being told it is possible that PPS could cripple them all over again. To me, that was just unfair.

Most doctors believe that PPS is the result of the damage polio did to the motor neurons, the nerves that stimulate the skeletal muscles. A healthy person has thousands of neurons, but as they age, some of the neurons cease to function. In the case of a polio patient, many of their motor neurons were destroyed during early stages of the disease leaving them with less motor neurons that function. So as a polio patient ages, at any moment, it is possible that most or all the neurons required to stimulate a particular muscle could cease to function.

But as polio survivors face their futures with grim determination, I learned that PPS would force me to accept reality. Unlike the Olympic athlete who worked out to an exhausted state, I would have to learn how to slow down once I started to tire out. Frankly, that would be the hardest part to deal with—the slowing down part. Not pushing myself to, and beyond, my physical limits was contrary to the way I had learned to succeed in life.

I cannot be sure if PPS was the cause of my muscle weakening because growing old also causes a weakening of the muscles.

Okay, so why not go to my doctor and ask him to make a PPS diagnosis?

A diagnosis of PPS is based on exclusion. The simple fact is that my doctor would evaluate my symptoms, medical history, and lab tests, and then, if the tests could not find any another cause, then he might diagnose PPS.

I chose to ignore the muscle weakening and continue to play golf twice a week and walk the eighteen hole course. A regulation length golf course equates to more than five miles of walking, so there is no question that my left leg and foot will be tired after completing a round of golf. Is my tiredness due to PPS? No one knows the answer to that question, but as Dr. Richard Owen of the Sister Kenny Institute states, "Only weight-lifters, racehorses, and 'old polios' run to total exhaustion."

I am now seventy-eight, and PPS or not, I still walk ten miles each week during my two games of golf. And when my muscles cannot handle the ten mile walk, I'll continue to play my favorite game because riding in a cart beats no golf at all.

Besides the more obvious disabilities that polio caused, there were some subtle wounds inflicted on those who survived polio.

Earlier, I chronicled that because I could not run as fast with my brace as the other boys, I was always picked last for the big kickball game during recess. But until I wrote this memoir, I had no idea of the level of personal shame I carried during the time I wore my brace. That realization took place as I dug through the photos taken of me during my polio years. In picture after picture, I found no photographic evidence that I had a brace on my left leg. Upon closer inspection of each photo, I saw that I had posed so my right leg covered my left leg, or my left pant leg had been pulled down to cover my left shoe. Not one photo, even in the heat of summer, ever showed me with my left leg exposed to the sun, or even a glint of steel from my brace. Only now do I comprehend that the embarrassment I felt as a child went far beyond being picked last for a game of kickball.

Recently, I talked with a friend whose mother had contracted polio as an adult. She recalled feeling embarrassed as she walked with her limping mother limp the local grocery store.

So the shame of a disability went far beyond the person who walked with a limp, or brace. It was very likely that the whole family, mine included, felt some embarrassment.

Few are aware that polio changed life for all disabled Americans by identifying the critical lack of access for the disabled.

By the late 1950s, the Salk vaccine had protected millions, but there were 450,000 polio survivors with varying degrees of disability who needed access to public buildings in order to get an education, or to make a living, and it did not take long for them to become frustrated by a lack of accessibility to their school or work. In fact, most viewed the lack of access as a form of discrimination. In the 1960s the use of a wheelchair in public was a daunting prospect—public transportation systems did not accommodate the disabled, and most buildings, including schools, were totally inaccessible to those with disabilities.

As the men, women, and children who had

become disabled by polio matured, they demanded the right to participate in the main stream of society. Polio survivors were in the forefront of the disability rights movement that emerged in the United States during the 1970s, and they helped to push legislation such as Section 504 of the Rehabilitation Act of 1973 to protect individuals from discrimination based on their disabilities.

Prior to the 1973 act, a disabled person in a wheelchair could not safely navigate across the street because there were no wheelchair curb cuts or ramps at intersections. They could not attend a multi-story elementary school, high school, or a university that did not offer elevators. They could not travel on their own via bus, airplane, or train. They could not gain access to a government building to apply for Social Security, or even spend a day watching Congress.

As I mentioned in a previous chapter, when I attempted to return for my eighth grade year at Audubon Jr. High School in 1951, the administration told my mom that if I could not navigate the stairs in the two story structure, I could not return to my old school. It was a classic example of a school discriminating against a disabled child.

The Rehabilitation Act of 1973 guaranteed that persons who were disabled could not be discriminated against within any program, service or activity where federal or other public revenues were used to provide and pay for that service.

That meant that if a disabled student attended college, high school, or any other public educational institution, the school had to come up with a way to accommodate that student. In other words, classes that were offered to non-disabled students must also be offered for those who were disabled.

The same was true for public transportation and access to public buildings such as town halls, national parks or public housing facilities. If tax dollars were involved, the disabled could not be denied access or service.

In 1977, four years after the passage of the Rehabilitation Act of 1973, the National Health Interview Survey reported that there were 254,000 persons living in the United States who struggled with deformed limbs, or other consequences of polio, and most required wheelchairs, crutches, leg braces, or breathing devices. It wasn't until the Carter administration took over in 1977 for the rules of Section 504 of the Rehabilitation Act to be implemented, opening up education and employment for all American children and adults with disabilities.

When I was nearly six, I was fitted for my first brace, a device that supported my left leg and foot. The brace was crafted from steel shafts attached to leather straps and it was permanently fastened to the sole of my left shoe.

During the decades of polio epidemics, hundreds of thousands of polio survivors required braces. Today, the world of orthotics still demands that a craftsman custom designs and constructs each brace, but the materials used are quite different.

In fact, the world of orthotics does not call such devices braces anymore. The proper term today is an orthosis.

An orthosis is generally used to control, guide, limit, and/or immobilize a body segment; or to restrict movement in a given direction., or to enhance movement in a given direction, or to aid rehabilitation after the removal of a cast, or to reduce pain. In other words, an orthosis can be built to do just about anything that is medically needed.

My newest orthosis is an ankle-foot orthosis (AFO) that supports my leg, ankle, and foot. AFOs are externally applied and intended to control position and motion of the ankle and compensate for weakness. AFOs are the most commonly prescribed orthosis, making up about 26% of all devices provided in the United States. According to a recent review of Medicare payment data the base cost of an AFO runs between $500 to $700.

My AFO is constructed of a lightweight polypropylene plastic in the shape of an "L", with the upright portion positioned behind my left calf and the lower portion running under my foot. The AFO is held to my calf with a velcro strap and was made to fit inside my golf shoes. My personalized AFO has a jointed ankle and was custom designed and manufactured from a positive model that was obtained from a negative plaster of Paris cast of my leg, ankle and foot. Since the plastic used to create the durable AFO must be heated to 400 °F, it makes direct molding of the plastic onto my left leg impossible.

So far, I only use my AFO when I walk eighteen holes of golf, or wear my heavy, black dress shoes while singing with my chorus. One of these days I will need to buy myself a pair of lighter weight black shoes so I will not have to wear my AFO while performing.

My AFO was custom made for me at Accolades, a local office that does Prosthetic and Orthotic design and manufacture. During my last visit, I talked with Chris Kerger, C.P., and marveled at how much lighter the plastic braces were when compared to the old ones made out of steel and leather.

He smiled. "Ken, you are different from most polios. I have some clients that will not accept braces made out of plastic and velcro, only those constructed of steel and leather."

"You're kidding. Why's that?"

"Who knows? In the world of orthotics, polios are known as the most stubborn patients in the world."

It was my turn to smile. "Chris, you need to remember that stubbornness was what got us polios through all those years of operations and hospitals. I hope you cut your clients a little slack."

"Trust me, Ken, I do."

Some years ago I was thrilled to learn that a major goal of the Rotary International Club was to eradicate polio worldwide.

To better understand the problems that Rotary would encounter, I did some research to find out what it took to eradicate smallpox.

The smallpox virus, like the polio virus, only survives in humans; therefore if one could vaccinate everyone in the world against smallpox, the virus would have no substrate in which to grow.

The last case of smallpox that occurred naturally happened in October, 1977, when a young man in Merka Town, Somalia, came down with the disease. He survived, and since then, no new cases of smallpox have been reported in Somalia or elsewhere in the world. In 1979, a global commission certified that smallpox had been eradicated, and this certification was officially accepted by the 33rd World Health Assembly in 1980.

Using the smallpox eradication as an example of what could be done, I looked into the Rotary International goal of eliminating polio in the world. What I found was missed target date after missed target date and I had to ask why. Wars, politics, and religion were the culprits. Successful vaccination programs require that medical teams enter an area where the polio virus exists and vaccinate the population, but vaccination teams are at risk. In 2013, six members of vaccination teams were murdered in Pakistan—Islamic extremist rebels in Somalia claimed that the polio vaccine caused AIDS—The Syrian government blocked efforts to distribute polio vaccine to opposition controlled areas of Syria.

As of mid-2015, however, the results are looking better. The world is closer then ever before to wiping out polio, with Africa reporting zero polio infections over the past eight months and only twenty-five cases identified in Pakistan and Afghanistan.

The experts remind us that progress against polio remains fragile, particularly in regions subject to instability. Two years ago, polio re-emerged in Syria after an absence of fourteen years.

Over time it became obvious that wiping out the polio virus would not be as easy as the removal of smallpox virus had been. Success should come in the near future because Rotary International, the World Health Organization, the Global Polio Eradication Initiative, the U. S. Centers of Disease Prevention, and the Bill and Melinda Gates Foundation have formed a strong coalition to complete the eradication of the polio virus within a few years. However, I am disappointed to report that as of September, 2016, two more cases of paralytic polio were discovered in Central Africa. The chilling part of this story is to remember was the fact that for every paralytic polio case occurs there are at least hundred cases of non-paralytic polio. In other words, the polio virus, in some areas of the world, continues to infect, paralyze, and kill, due to political, and civil turmoil.

Now, for the most exciting, and mind-boggling stories of *Polio and Me.*

In 2015, during a phase-one trial at Duke University, a polio virus, the same virus that killed and paralyzed millions, was used to destroy a glioblastoma, a fast growing, deadly, cancerous brain tumor that takes the lives of 12,000 Americans each year.

One of the world's leading cancer researchers, Dr. Henry Friedman, reported that an injection of the polio virus directly into the brain tumor either shrunk, or in a few cases completely eliminated the glioblastoma. Dr. Friedman was reluctant to use the word cure, but he felt that the Duke University trial might well be a turning point in cancer treatment.

And how did my old enemy become a friend? Dr. Matthias Gromeier, a molecular biologist, spent fifteen years in the lab reengineering the polio virus by replacing a genetic sequence with a harmless bit of cold virus to prevent the polio virus from reproducing in normal cells. Once his re-engineered polio virus entered a cancer cell, it released a toxin that broke down the wall that protects a cancer cell from a human's natural immune system. Following seven years of extensive safety studies, and after tests on 39 monkeys to prove they were free of polio, the FDA approved Gromeier's re-engineered polio virus for a Phase 1 trial on humans.

One of the trials' participants was a twenty-year-old woman named Stephanie Lipscomb. She had a glioblastoma tumor inside her head the size of a tennis ball. After surgery, radiation, and chemotherapy, her glioblastoma returned. At that point, Stephanie was only months from death and had nothing to lose, so she volunteered to become the first participant in the phase 1 trial. Gromeier's re-engineered polio virus was injected directly into Stephanie's tumor and the polio virus attached itself to the surface of the cells that made up her glioblastoma. Because Stephanie was the first participant in the trial, no one knew what to expect next. The doctors thought it was possible the polio virus might do some good but they had no idea what would happen over time.

At first, there appeared to be an increase in the size of the tumor, but an MRI showed that the tumor had not been growing. Instead,

Stephanie's immune system had come to her defense and five months after the polio virus injection, the glioblastoma was actually shrinking.

Dr. Gromeier believes that once the polio virus infected the tumor, it broke down the tumor's protective shield and enabled Stephanie's immune system to attack the glioblastoma. During the ensuing twenty-one months, her tumor continued to shrink and today it looks to be gone from her brain. At this point of her life, Stephanie is cancer free.

A Phase 1 study is only designed to determine the correct dosage for a drug or a therapy, so the phase 1 team was surprised and overjoyed with her progress.

Since Stephanie's success, there have been twenty-two participants in the Phase 1 trial. Eleven died. Most of those were given a higher dose of the polio virus. But even the eleven that died lived months longer than expected. The other eleven continue to improve. Four have lived longer than six months, a huge advancement for patients with a glioblastoma tumor. Two have lived nearly three years, unheard of in patients who have been diagnosed with that form of cancer.

Dr. Gromeier has tested his re-engineered polio virus against a number of other cancers and has been able, in a lab dish, to kill off lung cancers, breast cancers, colorectal cancers, prostate cancers, pancreatic cancers, liver cancers, and renal cancers.

Dr. Peter Marks, the FDA deputy director responsible for monitoring hundreds of experimental treatments for cancer, has expressed concern that sometimes the first participant treated with an experimental therapy could respond better than later participants. Even he agrees that the emerging field of immunotherapy is exciting and some immunotherapy's have allowed cancer patients to live much longer.

Next year the FDA could grant Duke what's called "breakthrough status" which would make the polio virus treatment available to more patients much sooner.

Okay, now you can sit back, relax, and unbuckle your seat belt. Your seven-decade journey on the Polio Time Machine is complete and you have returned to the present. I trust you learned some interesting facts during your trip.

Before you go, I want to consider a line of thought that I had avoided over those decades because the query would force me to face the unknown: What my life would have been like had I not caught polio in 1943?

Here are my thoughts, and feel free to offer further questions, or conclusions if you think I have missed some.

As you will recall, during my initial polio infection, the growth in my left leg had stopped and I eventually ended up with a three-inch difference between my left and right leg. So off the bat, in my theoretical, non-polio existence, I would have ended up three inches taller—a strapping six-foot-tall young man with sandy-red hair and a few freckles.

Okay, so I would have grown taller, but in what other way could my life have been different?

It is possible that my mom might not have needed to go to work. But World War Two, and the social/economic female revolution (some call it the Rosie-the-Riveter revolution) would have happened regardless of my polio, so it's possible that my mom would have gone to work just to keep up with the times.

What about my relationship with my brother and sister? The three of us would have gone to the same junior and senior high schools, and each would have received his or her full share of love and attention that every child deserves. I'm positive that my brother, sister and I would have had many more shared experiences and would have been much closer as the three of us worked and played our way toward adulthood.

Without polio would I have attended that legendary party where I met the young woman who became the love of my life?

The answer to that question is easy. In my polio life, we attended different high schools so the odds of us ever meeting, much less dating were very small. However, in my life without polio, Arlene and I would have both attend Dorsey High School and I am positive that one day, destiny would have seated us at the same table during lunch. While munching our peanut butter and jam sandwiches, I would have glanced up, looked into her stunning blue eyes, and with the boldness of a confident sandy-haired, six-foot-tall dude, I would ask her if she wanted to go to a movie the next weekend. She would have smiled, thought for a moment for propriety's sake, nodded her head, and then said yes.

During our time at Dorsey, we would have attended football games and danced at our proms. Years later, we would have become engaged and eventually married just like we did in my polio life.

Next, did my polio act as a wedge between my parents, a separation that would eventually lead to divorce? I feel that polio or not, my mom and dad's marriage would have ended up on the rocks because of their irreconcilable social and economic differences. Real life is not like the old movies where two people who grew up on different sides of the tracks marry and live happily ever after. In my opinion, every time my family went to Grandma and Grandpa

Bardeen's fancy Hollywood house, my mom was reminded of the life she had left behind. That was a far bigger wedge pushing my mom and dad apart than my polio ever was.

Would I have liked school? This question is not quite as easy to answer, but by attending all my classes on a regular basis and not falling so far behind the other kids, I am sure that my opinion of school would have improved. Also, I am positive my self-esteem would not have suffered from being the only kid in school who wore high-top leather shoes with a brace and a three-inch heel. Who knows, I might have ended up on a list of polio survivor overachievers like:

Itzhak Perlman—A virtuoso violinist.

Frida Kahlo—An artist renown for her paintings.

Francis Ford Coppola—Movie director, producer, and screenwriter.

Wilma Rudolph—First American woman to win three Olympic gold medals.

Benjamin C. Bradlee—Executive Editor of the Washington Post.

Elsie MacGill—The first female aircraft designer in the world.

From a violin virtuoso to the first female aircraft designer in the world, polio inspired many to achieve lofty goals.

Would I have played sports? Yes, and the

more the merrier. I love baseball, basketball, and football and with any luck, I would have tried out for all three sports in high school. With even more luck, I would have learned early on that football is a very dangerous game and would have gotten out before I permanently hurt myself.

Would I have attended college? Again, not an easy question to answer. I am not sure because my family did not have the tradition of earning four-year college degrees. After my sister Pat's high school graduation, she was done with her formal education, but she told me that mom and dad never encouraged her to further her education. My brother did take some junior college classes, but unlike my dad, he did not complete his AA degree. For myself, if I had my life to live over (even with polio), I would have tried to attend a university. As I grow older, I find that I am eager to learn from lectures and extension college classes, and lately, through the Osher Life Long Learning Institute (OLLI) out of Sonoma State University. OLLI gives people like myself the opportunity to learn for the joy of learning..

And what about my growth into an adult living in our world? Did I make it through my eleven-year bout of polio with my sanity intact? When I was four, I was known to have had terrible fits of anger and would throw a temper tantrum to get my way. According to my mom and dad, I was a difficult child. Somehow, I had figured out how to let my anger out in a grocery store, or a doctor's office, or church. I would scream, stamp my feet, and hold my breath until my parents would give in to whatever was bugging me at that particular moment. Based on my parents description of me as a stubborn four-year-old, I am not sure how I would have turned out as an adult without polio. But I do know that all those four-year-old temper tantrums dissipated like the morning fog during my hellish eleven-year ride on the polio roller-coaster.

As I conclude this memoir, it is hard for me to believe that it has been more than sixty years since I walked across the stage at Westchester High School to accept my diploma.

A few years later, Arlene and I were married and we raised three wonderful children: Lorry, Hugh, and Wendy. Not too many more years passed before we were handing out advice on how to raise our four grandchildren, and today, it seems to me that we spend most of our leisure hours happily wrapping birthday presents for our nine great-grandchildren.

All that joy and happiness came from two people—a little boy who, at five and a half years, could not stand or walk, and a beautiful, blue-eyed girl who would become his bride of fifty-eight years.

I have no doubt that the years I spent recovering from polio have made me mentally stronger. Along with that toughness, I am proud to say, came real compassion for those who were less fortunate than I, such as the little girl in the iron lung, or my friend Juan, or the boy with cerebral palsy we called the Spaz.

Thanks to Doctor Lowman, and my mom, wherever you are, I still walk with a normal gait, and stand ready to take on the next challenge.

One final thought. There are a few parents in this world who feel that vaccinations could, or will, harm their children. To them I pose this question: Would you rather expose them to the far greater risk of contracting a disease like polio? Or how about Measles?

Here is a fact concerning measles that I hope will act as a wake-up call to those parents who refuse to vaccinate their children. Recent studies have shown that once a child contracts measles it takes from two to three years for that child's immune system to return to normal. That means after contracting measles, your child will be far more susceptible to infection from other illnesses, even the poliovirus, for up to three years.

In the opinion of one man who lived through polio, not vaccinating your children is the same as telling them to ignore the red light at a busy intersection. They may make it across the street once, maybe twice, but sooner or later they will be rundown, and perhaps even die.

Trust me, the futures of your precious child is not worth that risk.

Authors Notes

Most readers would think that writing the "my life" section of this book would be easy. To some extent, the reader would be correct. But many memories were added to, or reinforced, by my dad, mom, sister, brother, aunts, uncles, cousins, and nieces.

To write the unbelievable story of discovering the first polio vaccine was more daunting than I had expected. To come up with many of the obscure facts, I found some of the information in the State of California data base dating back to the 1930s. But most of my information came from interviews with doctors, nurses, physical therapists, and orthotic specialists.

Although the clinic, and the third floor Boy's ward at The Orthopedic Hospital where I spent my childhood years are long gone, the Orthopedic Hospital is still alive and well with a new hospital in Santa Monica. The organization joined with UCLA and formed the Orthopedic Institute for Children where they continue to offer needed medical care, education, and research. On the site of "my" old hospital sits The OIC Ambulatory Surgery Center, the region's first stand-alone facility specifically designed to only provide outpatient orthopaedic surgical care to children. With two operating rooms, and six pre- and post-surgical suites, it will help to reduce surgery wait times for children in need of orthopaedic surgery.

To help me to continue to pay back some of the life changing medical care I received at the Orthopedic Hospital, I will donate, to the Orthopedic Institute for Children, 50% of the royalties from the sale of each paperback book, and 25% of the royalties from the sale of each Kindle book.

If you are seeking a speaker for your service club, or want me to discuss the polio years with your eight grade class, or invite me to talk about *Polio and Me* at your book club, please email me at ken@kendalton.com

One final thought. If you have children, or grandchildren, or great-grandchildren, buy a copy of this book and read it to them out loud. The kids will love the stories and learn about the past while you will have the opportunity to cry or chuckle as you read to them.

Selected Bibliography

The History of the Los Angeles County Hospital- 1878-1968— Helen Eastman Martin—University of Southern California Press—©1979

Polio's Legacy—Edmund J. Sass—University Press of America—© 1996

Polio, An American Story—David M. Oshinsky—Oxford Unikversity Press—© 2005

Living With Polio—Daniel J.Wilson—University of Chicago Press—© 2005

Patenting the Sun: Polio and the Salk Vaccine—Jane Smith—William Morrow & Co—© 1990

Time Magizine, August 23, 1954

Los Angeles Times, November 9, 1997

https://sites.google.com/site/abasioinfo/Home/history

http://www.ninds.nih.gov/disorders/foot_drop/foot_drop.htm

http://www.historynet.com/v-j-day-1945-the-world-rejoices.htm

Physiotherapy Review, 1945:25:79

http://www.comminit.com/polio/node/185038

www.surgeryencyclipedia.com–2014

The Albert Sabin Obituary-New Your Times-March 4, 1993

The Jonas Salk Obituary-New York Times-June 24, 1995

Newsweek, Karen Bartlett, November, 28, 2014

The History of the Los Angeles Orthopedic Hospital, 1911 to 2011

63198202R00159

Made in the USA
Charleston, SC
30 October 2016